SEO

BLACK BOOK

A GUIDE TO THE SEARCH ENGINE OPTIMIZATION INDUSTRY'S SECRETS

R.L. Adams

All Rights Reserved

FTC & Legal Notices

This Page Intentionally Left Blank

CONTENTS

This Page Intentionally Left Blank

WHAT IS SEO?

To be successful in today's Internet marketplace, you must have a complete understanding of Google's search and the components involved in optimizing a site for your keywords. By developing this ability to rank at the top of search engine results pages you not only command social creditability, but you also gain a huge competitive edge.

The practice of Search Engine Optimization (SEO) is the set of methods, techniques and principles utilized by search engine marketers (SEMs) to increase the relevancy ranking of a Website.

SEO has evolved into a multi-faceted business with various approaches from social media, to On-Site Optimization, Off-Site Optimization, content building, and everything in between. While seemingly daunting at first for beginners, as your SEO knowledge expands and grows, you'll gain more of an inherent understanding and reasoning for how Google's search works, and how to improve any listing on its ranking pages.

It's difficult to organically rank yourself for any Google

search results page, let alone at the top of page one. Some search keywords have become incredibly difficult to rank for resulting in a lot of frustration and discouragement for most people who attempt to practice SEO. This is because, the search engine industry has itself been built upon an element of disinformation. Search engines with their complex and secrecy shrouded algorithms are pressing for more and more relevant search results, while SEMs are working harder and harder to keep their sites relevant.

Developing and refining a talent for SEO can mean riches and fortunes to anyone lucky enough to perfect the craft. The potential to have your site and content exposed, organically, to millions of potential consumers through SERPs is tremendous. The sheer volume of commerce and the potential for upside with SEO draw millions of people intrigued by the trade each and every year.

In journeying to understand the industry and how the search engines, and more notably, Google's search, works, I've come across countless books, blog posts, comments, forum threads, and eBooks that tout the secrets of winning the Google search game. But in the end, in my opinion, most books either provide partial or outdated information that leaves the complete picture of ranking at the top of SERPs incomplete.

My purpose for you in this book is to deliver my knowledge and allow you to have a complete look inside at what it takes to make real and lasting advances on SERPs. In this book, I'll walk you through both, the foundational basics of SEO, and some advanced strategies being implemented by the high traffic builders that you'll be hard pressed to find elsewhere in a book like this. As you come to see the bigger picture, you'll understand the components involved in ranking at the top of SERPs, and be able to harness that information to your advantage.

You'll have the tools and knowledge to begin implementing to improve the rankings for any Website in today's competitive search engine environment. This competitive edge will help start or continue your career as an SEO mastermind.

WHO THIS BOOK IS FOR

Written for anyone with an insatiable desire to learn the ins and outs of the Google SEO world, this book is the culmination of experience that I have gathered over the course of over a decade of grueling work in the SEO field.

I have researched, tested, and studied just about every method and technique possible for ranking on Google and other search engines, and this book is the culmination of much of that information. This is not a book for anyone who isn't absolutely serious and committed to learning the real industry methods, and techniques for propelling yourself up Google's search rankings.

In this SEO book I provide a lot of the foundational concepts that allow you to rank your pages and sites at the top of SERPs while also providing step-by-step instructions in some sections on how to conduct the techniques. In the pages to follow you'll come to learn some of the true, tried, and proven techniques that work, today, for Google SEO improvement. With the recent major amendments and overhauls to Google's search engine algorithm, this book is a necessity for anyone looking to stay ahead of the Google Panda & Penguin curve.

If you commit to reading this book from end to end I assure you that you will not only become proficient in the SEO trade, but you'll achieve master level at a very accelerated pace. While going through the process of learning SEO I was unable to find a single repository containing the type and style of information that I disseminate in this book. These real world practices contained in the pages of this book are not filled with "fluff" and filler to occupy unnecessary space, but rather real usable techniques to ranking on Google's SERPs.

In the SEO trade, most techniques and tips are guarded and protected heavily as the sheer nature of the culture has been to shroud itself in secrecy for want of keeping prying potential competitors away. Most resources and books on SEO will leave out key information and steps that are critical to the overall success of any SEO campaign. Without some of this basic foundational knowledge you may find yourself at a plateau very early on, wondering why you're not having the results you were expecting.

INTRODUCTION

The evolution of the Internet has been remarkable to watch. Over the past decade, the exponential rise of both the power and reach of the Internet has been breathtaking. This once small array of computers has now spawned into a global network of billions of Web pages located on servers across the globe, accessible anytime, anywhere, by anyone.

A virtual super highway providing access to the world's consumers, the importance of a powerful presence on the Web has become a necessity in today's competitive business environment, and no longer an option. No company has played a larger role in the construction and development of that virtual superhighway than Google, building the foundation of its entire business on our desires to seek out and find information through online search.

Once operating out of a small room on the Stanford

University campus, Google has now spawned into a multibillion dollar, Multinational Corporation, with virtual tentacles reaching far and wide. The idea for the company came about when Stanford University PhD students Sergey Brin and Larry Page began a research project to improve Internet search. Creating an algorithm that would use backlinks and page rank as its primary source of ranking for Websites, Brin and Page revolutionized the search industry, as we know it, launching their company Google in the process.

The Google search algorithm was released to spider the Web in 1996, searching out links to Websites, gauging their importance and simultaneously attributing a relevancy ranking to each site in the process. The Google search algorithm and the company itself, has come a long way since the early days of its birth, exhibiting tremendous growth stretching even beyond the wildest dreams of its co-founders.

The Company has now made the word "Google" synonymous with search. This brand awareness of the search giant rivals some of the world's largest corporations such as McDonald's and Coca-Cola, extending its name into the very depths of every country, state, city, municipality and residential acre of the world.

Considering the scope and importance of the Internet and its search today, being found online is more important now than ever, and businesses are doing whatever it takes in order to ensure that they appear relevant in search results. With the increase in competition and accessibility of the Internet to virtually anyone, it's no surprise that the level of difficulty in attaining high organic search rankings has drastically increased over time.

With billions of pages constantly vying for the coveted number one spots on search engine results pages (SERPs), an entire industry has sprung up dedicated to the craft of search engine optimization. The race for presence on these SERPs has been driven not only by competition in the marketplace as the Internet has grown, but also by Google's desire to make its search results more and more relevant and accurate over time, forcing Websites and search engine marketers to work harder and harder to stay ahead of the curve.

As Google's search algorithms have aged and evolved, the industry has changed and shifted dramatically in order to adapt, and staying relevant is more important now than ever. A company or product's appearance at the top of SERPs can have a significant impact on its bottom line. With access to such a large market of global consumers, it's no surprise why so many people are striving for the type of attention that only a top organic search result can bring.

FUTURE UPDATES

While I have taken every precaution to provide you with as much current information as possible related to SEO practices and the industry, it's important to understand that with the inherent nature of the industry's fast pace for change, some of the information in this book may be outdated by the time you're reading it. However, this book will be updated periodically to reflect information as it evolves so you can rest assured that you will be reading the most current information readily available.

This book has been written as a post Google Panda & Google Penguin guide to ranking at the top of Google search results, and while I cannot guarantee that you will be able to rank #1 for any given search result, if you follow the guidelines suggested in this book, and put in the honest effort that SEO requires, you will see dramatic improvements in virtually any keyword for virtually any site.

If you're unfamiliar with Google's Panda & Penguin

updates, these were changes to the search giant's algorithm that sought to increase the relevancy of its search results. While punishing poor low-quality content sites that learned how to bend the rules to reach top rankings on Google, it rewarded high-quality, rich-content sites providing tremendous value and information to its visitors.

Of course, there are always the exceptions to the rule here for being able to achieve top rankings on Google's SERPs. As you may already know, if you're attempting to do SEO for sites that include gambling, pornography, or other illegal prescription products, you are going to see heavy amounts of resistance in ranking high, if at all.

1

SEO CRASH COURSE

Search Engine Optimization, or SEO for short, has grown into a vast industry encompassing a variety of diverse tasks & techniques. What started out as a simple job at first, has evolved into a labor-intensive, multi-faceted nearly full-time occupation. Stretching from keyword research, to content creation, On-Site optimization, Off-Site optimization, and social media marketing, amongst other efforts, SEO has become an enormous undertaking.

In a search environment with a constantly evolving algorithm, it's important for marketers to stay current and stay relevant. By understanding what it takes to rank at the top of the Google's SERPs today and into the future, you can create a strategy and approach that will produce long-term results and not just temporary gains.

In the SEO industry, content is king, and as ruler of the Web, special attention needs to be paid to the quality of content distributed in association with any Website or page. Gone are the days when marketers could put out low-quality content spun in a hundred different directions and spread across all corners of the Web in hopes that it would bolster search engine rankings for their sites. Today, trying to cheat Google with low-quality content, link schemes, and poor user browsing experiences, will see you drop like a ship's anchor in the rankings.

Over the course of the past several years Google has cracked down on these so-called content farms that produce low-quality, poorly researched content that contain massive amounts of outbound links. By releasing its Google Panda algorithm update, and more recently, its Google Penguin algorithm update, Google has sent a clear message to the world. These two algorithm updates created a massive restructuring and shuffling of SERP rankings, demoting pages with low-quality, poorly researched content, while promoting those with high-quality, well-researched content.

The rise of social media platforms in recent years, has also given way to significant changes and improvements in search engine algorithms. Successful SEO strategies today must embrace social media platforms by having their content shared and liked as frequently and by as many people as possible.

Social media's role in search relevancy has seen a dramatic rise due to the large part that it now plays in our lives. By liking or sharing a piece of content, you're indicating the relevancy of it to Google and the other search engines, and they've begun to take notice. Algorithms have been adjusted and modified to reflect backlinks coming from popular social media sites and they now factor into the relevancy score of a search listing.

With all of these different elements playing a part in SEO, how do you go about creating a winning strategy that weaves together all of the diverse approaches that are required for a successful SEO campaign today? By first understanding all of the different parts and components that are involved with ranking a site, you'll come to embrace and comprehend an industry that may at first seem overwhelmingly difficult and complex.

Any successful endeavor starts with gaining an understanding for the knowledge associated with it. In the SEO industry, that knowledge required is vast and spread out across various different mediums, so it's important to absorb and understand what's involved in search rankings, then set out to implement those practices while gauging your results to determine successes. You'll be wearing a lot of hats, so be prepared to invest some time in creating a winning strategy that works for you.

This book is broken up into sections based on the parts and components involved in the practice of SEO. At the back of the book is an appendix filled with a glossary of terms related to the SEO industry and various SEO practices. It's recommended that you review and understand the terms in the appendix and use it as a reference for any terms you may not completely grasp in the book.

Fully executing a successful SEO campaign involves understanding and implementing the practices taught in this book. To implement some of these practices you'll need to have the proper tools in your SEO arsenal. Attempting to conduct SEO without the use of these tools would be like trying to run a car without gasoline; it simply won't work.

Keep in mind that SEO also requires patience, and in order to be successful you'll need to implement these practices consistently, taking daily action in order to achieve the results you're after. Most successful campaigns for SEO take at least 90 days to see the biggest gains.

Although you may begin seeing some SEO results within shorter periods of time the largest long term gains will not be visible until at least 60 to 90 days from the time you performed your SEO work. Due to the fact that Google does multiple updates of its search results, through quick re-indexing of listings that tend to shuffle SERP listings around a lot at first but settle in after longer periods of time have elapsed and deep-indexing has occurred.

The amount of time that will be required for you to see gains in your particular SEO projects will vary for each keyword based on the level of competition and the search volume. The key is to stay focused and stay determined. By keeping your eye on the prize of top rankings, within time you'll be successful, as long as you don't give up.

TOOLING UP

SEO requires a set of tools of the trade that you'll need in order to build and manage an effective optimization strategy. These tools will automate certain tasks such as link building that may otherwise be impossible to do in the volumes required within any respectable time constraint when done manually. Just as a carpenter has a hammer and a saw that are essential to his trade, an SEO specialist has his own set of tools that are needed to launch and manage any effective optimization effort.

It's important to follow along with the steps while utilizing the tools mentioned in order to achieve any success in SEO. The gains you stand to reap by employing the tools discussed versus the small investment needed for some of them are phenomenal. A top-tier search result can rake in countless income for any product or service so ensure that you've tooled up to get the job done in order to propel your listing to the top of SERPs.

KEYWORD RESEARCH

[handwritten: called Keyword Planner now]

✓ **Google Adwords Keyword Tool** – The majority of your keyword research will be done using the Google Adwords Keyword Tool, a free online resource provided by the search giant itself to aid advertisers with potential ad campaigns. However, you don't need to run an ad campaign in order to use the Keyword Tool, and you don't even need to have a Google account. Although, it is much simpler to use the Keyword Tool with a Google account by not having to answer the Captcha challenge question each time a search is performed. You can find the Google Adwords Keyword Tool at the following link: https://adwords.google.com/o/KeywordTool

✓ **SEO Quake Browser Plug-in** – The SEO Quake plug-in is a free downloadable plug-in available for Firefox, or as an extension available for the Chrome browser, that allows you to see information related to a domain that's critical to keyword rankings. You can set your preferences in this tool, turning on and off various pieces of data that come through and it's a great resource to quickly check competitors' domain ages, number of inbound links, Alexa rankings, number of Twitter Tweets, number of Facebook Likes, and number of Google Plus Ones, quickly while performing these searches on Google. You can find the SEO Quake Plug-In at the following link: http://www.seoquake.com

WEBSITE DEVELOPMENT

Wordpress – With near 60 million installations as of the writing of this book, Wordpress is certainly a blogging and Website development platform to be reckoned with. To most people starting out that don't understand complex programming languages, Wordpress offers a very simple and easy to use platform.

The Wordpress system enables you to get your site up and running fast allowing you to concentrate on your SEO efforts sooner as opposed to going down the traditional route of hiring a Web designer or doing it yourself. With Wordpress you can quickly install a theme to modify the design of your site, upload a logo, create title tags, and do much of the On-Site SEO work discussed in Chapter 4 of this book.

Additionally, if you are a seasoned developer or Web designer, then you can further harness and use the power of Wordpress as an initial platform for your site. Furthermore, if you're passing the site off to a client, they'll have a built-in online system they can utilize to manage Web pages and blog posts even after the project is complete.

To setup Wordpress with a hosting company on your own domain use either **GoDaddy.com** or **Hostgator.com.** Both companies provide excellent managed Wordpress hosting packages.

TRAFFIC STATISTICS & TRACKING

Google Analytics – The most sophisticated Website analytics engine on the market today, Google Analytics offers free Website analytics to any site looking to integrate a small piece of code into its pages for tracking & analysis. Of course, tracking and analysis is an important component to analyzing SEO efforts and having a good system you can utilize to track your Website's traffic is paramount to understanding just how effective those SEO efforts have been. You can find Google Analytics at the following link: http://www.google.com/analytics

Google Analyticator Wordpress Plug-in – If you're working with the Wordpress platform, then once you have your Google Analytics account all setup, setting up this plug-in will help link your Website with your analytics account. By utilizing this plug-in you won't have to manually add any code to your site, the synch will happen seamlessly through the Wordpress administration platform. You can find Google Analyticator at the following link: http://bit.ly/analyticator

Piwik – This is another powerful Website analytics platform that provides a bit more detail than Google Analytics does, but it's also more complex to initially setup if you're not familiar with installing a PHP application on your server. Piwik provides more real, down to the last detail, information about your visitors, that Google doesn't provide due to privacy policies it has in place. You can find Piwik at the following link: http://piwik.org

ON-SITE SEO

SEO for Wordpress Plug-in – On-Site SEO can be overwhelming at times, however, having the proper SEO plug-ins can make all the difference if you're using a publishing platform like Wordpress. The SEO for Wordpress plug-in is one of the best free plug-ins that I've found for Wordpress, allowing you to update the meta description tag, title tag, and analyze other On-Site SEO data for each specific page or article post through its interface. You can find the plugin at the following link: http://wordpress.org/extend/plugins/wordpress-seo/

SEOPressor Wordpress Plug-in – SEOPressor is another great plug-in for Wordpress that provides you with page specific SEO content scoring, relaying a breakdown of your SEO score based out of 100 percent for any given keyword you select. This plug-in is being used by over 125,000 Wordpress Websites and is terrific if you want to take a lot of the guesswork out of your On-Site SEO. You can find SEOPressor at the following link: http://bit.ly/seopressorv5

OFF-SITE SEO

✓? **TribePro** – This is probably one of the best online applications for instantly dropping hundreds if not thousands of high page rank backlinks through social media instantly from a single share. Tribepro syndicates your content to all the people who have selected to syndicate you in your tribe on all the social networks they have activated. You can quickly build up to 5,000 high page rank backlinks to your URL on networks like Facebook, Twitter, Google Plus, MySpace, Friend Free, and 43 other social networks. You can find TribePro at the following link: http://bit.ly/powerofthetribe

Onlywire – Onlywire is a content syndication platform that's utilized by Tribepro and it can syndicate your content on autopilot to up to 48 social networks. There's some initial setup involved in getting your various social media accounts established, however, once you're up and going it's relatively simple to use.

When used in connection with Tribepro, it will syndicate your content and anyone else's content in your tribe that you've chosen to syndicate. This application is an absolute must for anyone serious about SEO. You can find Onlywire at the following link: http://bit.ly/onlywirelink

Fiverr – This Website is an excellent way to speed up your Off-Site SEO link building. The concept behind this site is based around vendors willing to provide a multitude of different services for as little as $5 USD. A terrific resource for finding and hiring vendors willing to do all sorts of Off-Site SEO link building work, Fiverr will become an invaluable online destination for your Off-Site SEO work. Whether you're hiring vendors to create link wheels, link pyramids, or perform other Off-Site SEO work, Fiverr is simple to use and excellent for hiring individuals to help boost SEO presence for any site.

Pingler – Pingler is a Website dedicated to setting up and pinging a specific URL on a periodic basis. Pinging is part of the Off-Site SEO process and tells Google to visit and revisit a link based on the amount of time specified (usually every 3 days). When you use Pingler, you'll know that Google's spiders will quickly visit the content that you've placed online indexing and revisiting it based on the time period you specify.

You can ping links for free with Pingler, however it's best to sign up for one of their basic accounts that will let you track and re-ping your links automatically without having to return and re-enter them yourself every few days.

Linklicious – During the process of creating low-level links in mass quantity you'll be working hard to make, you'll need a way to ensure these links are indexed and pinged in high volume. The best service to conduct this volume pinging is with Linklicious. Since Google doesn't crawl 95% of the low page rank and no page rank links out there, you have to tell it to do so if you want those links to count in Google's algorithm. Without doing this, you're wasting your precious time and resources creating links that may never get crawled and indexed.

Linklicious offers a free account that allows you to ping up to 2,500 links per day, a Basic account that allows you to ping up to 10,000 links per day, and a Pro account that allows you to ping up to 50,000 links per day. Providing you with a high quality drip-feed system to send your links to Google in an organic looking fashion, Linklicious is a must for any SEO campaign. Without the usage of a drip-feed system like the one provided by Linklicious, mass pinging of links to Google in a short time span will get your listing demoted, and even de-indexed in some extreme cases; caught up in the Google Sandbox nightmare. You can find Linklicious at the following link: http://bit.ly/linkliciousme

SOCIAL MEDIA MARKETING

Empire Avenue – Empire Avenue is an excellent resource for bringing together all of your social media platforms into one place and allowing you to collaborate with other like-minded marketers that are using social media to spread and share each other's content. On Empire Avenue you can connect any number of social networks that you are participating in to the service and begin collaborating with other online marketers working to boost their SEO and social media statuses.

As a tradable commodity, your account on Empire Avenue becomes a fictitious stock on the site, earning you the Website's own currency called Eaves when your shares are purchased. While it's a fictional trading platform, the site is excellent for collaborating and doing missions with other people to either share their content or have them share yours in exchange for Eaves.

Empire Avenue is a free site, however you can always purchase more Eaves when you run dry or just do missions to earn them for free. This is an excellent way to get real human people to collaborate with, Facebook Share, like, Google Plus One, and Re-Tweet your content, all excellent sources of SEO link juice.

Twitter – Twitter is an excellent platform for getting yourself out there and noticed by just about anyone. With a page rank of 9 out of 10, Twitter backlinks can be very powerful link juice when pointing to your site's pages. If you don't already have a Twitter account for yourself or your business, then set one up and make it look professional.

Since the Twitter account is a reflection of you and your business, don't ruin it by posting unprofessional tweets or photos. Select a quality photo, and pick a pleasing background that's easy on the eyes and ensure that you create a backlink to your Website in your Twitter profile.

Facebook – With over one billion people on Facebook, this is probably the best way to network, socialize and create high quality Off-Site SEO backlinks on a regular basis. Create a professional looking page for your business and ensure that you hyperlink your domain name in your profile. Each time you add content share it on Facebook to pick up more of those high page-ranking links back to your site.

When setting up a business or fan page on Facebook, keep it professional, because remember, this is a reflection of you as well. If you're doing this for a client, get them to setup the page and make you an admin so that you can adjust the appearance, setup the company profile with Website link, and begin sharing content directly on the page for more high-quality backlinks.

Google Plus – The importance and reach of Google's own social network, Google Plus, has grown tremendously over the past couple of years. Today, having a Google Plus profile is not an option, it's a must, and being in as many circles as possible will increase the prominence of any content tied to your author account on Google's SERPs.

YouTube – Google loves YouTube videos. Maybe it's because the search giant owns the video powerhouse, but for whatever reason, creating videos on YouTube will explode your SEO presence when linked to your content.

By shooting & uploading videos that provide value, such as instructional videos and how-to videos that solve problems, you will be able to quickly move to the top of Google SERPs. By having a popular video on YouTube with a link back to your content or embedded in your content, you create a winning strategy for increased rankings.

Shareaholic Wordpress Plug-in – A terrific free Wordpress plug-in, Shareaholic allows your content to be easily shared across any number of social networks by visitors to your site or blog. Shareaholic sets up simple sharing capabilities on your Wordpress-based Website's pages and posts allowing the content to be very easily shared amongst dozens of social networks. http://wordpress.org/extend/plugins/sexybookmarks/

CREATING A SUCCESSFUL SEO STRATEGY

Creating and implementing a successful SEO strategy takes a sincere amount of effort. It requires daily and consistent action with link building, unique content creation, social media marketing, along with other On-Site and Off-Site SEO efforts. If you're not absolutely committed to an SEO project, you might see it fail if you can't follow through with these tasks on a daily basis.

Think of your site as a plant, and SEO as the water and sunlight; without water and sunlight a plant can't grow and flourish to its full potential, and will eventually wither away and die. By providing the proper amount of nourishment each and everyday, however, your plant will grow little by little until the day it fully blooms and blossoms.

Much like a plant, your listing will climb the SERPs little by little each day as more work is done to it until one day when it shoots to the top and your hard work pays off. While getting to the #1 position involves a lot of hard work and is never guaranteed, making sure that you stay there also includes basic daily actions as well; your work is not completely finished even when you reach the top.

Covering foundational SEO strategies, along with some advanced ranking techniques, this book, when read end to end will allow you to conduct a successful White-Hat SEO campaign for any site or page. If you follow along with the processes and steps laid out in this book, you will be able to successfully improve your SERP ranking for virtually any search keyword. Here is an overview of the process and steps laid out in this book for effectually instituting a successful SEO campaign.

Chapter 2 – Securing an Aged Domain

Part of what Google sees as relevant is finding a domain name that has some age and history to it. The search giant understands that businesses are vying to climb its rankings, but it also understands that new businesses are less relevant than existing businesses that have been in existence for some time.

Like any business that has been around for years, an aged domain is a domain that has more credibility, and this is the view taken by Google. An aged domain is a domain that has been indexed in the past two or more years by Google and is considered a trusted domain. Even if the domain name is old, it must have been indexed and have had some activity in the past to be considered an aged domain name.

Chapter 3 – Conducting Effective Keyword Research

Your site or page's primary keyword is at the heart of your SEO strategy and all your other activities will revolve around it. As the main target of search queries, the primary keyword for both your site or a specific piece of content located anywhere on the Internet, is going to be what you focus all your other SEO efforts on. Doing the proper research at this stage of the game will set yourself up for success moving forward.

Chapter 4 – On-Site SEO Techniques

Having excellent On-Site (or On-Page) SEO will give your site that much needed boost and potential to rank at the top of SERPs. If your On-Site SEO is lacking, then your capability to rank high will diminish greatly.

In this section we'll discuss what matters today for search engines when it comes to optimizing your pages with On-Site SEO techniques. These techniques will drastically improve your end results and make all your other efforts that much more worthwhile.

Chapter 5 – Setting up Website Analytics & Keyword Tracking

Setting up a good system for analysis and tracking will allow you to determine the success of your SEO efforts. There are only a handful of good tools that are available on the market today for tracking site usage and statistics. In SEO, there are multiple different tracking and analysis tools that can be used. The most important elements you'll want to keep track of will be keyword searches and sources of your Website's traffic.

Chapter 6 – Creating Unique, Well-Researched Content

A cornerstone of any successful SEO campaign, we'll discuss what it takes to write well-researched unique content. Since writing well researched, unique content is critical to ranking high on Google's SERPs, this is something that should be an important focus for you.

If you're unable to write well, or you feel like your English may not be perfect, then you may consider outsourcing some of this work. Although, since writing good content is so vital to SEO, and something you'll need to be doing on a consistent basis, getting very good at this one major component could mean drastic differences in your ranking success rates.

Chapter 7 – Off-Site SEO Techniques

Link relationships are a foundational part of the Internet and its search algorithms. However, making mistakes and being severely penalized by Google for some types of link building activities are some of the pitfalls you'll need to avoid. Understanding what works and what doesn't when it comes to Off-Site SEO is important to give your site that push it needs to get found, noticed, and appear relevant to search engines.

Without the proper Off-Site SEO guidance you may be unknowingly practicing Black-Hat SEO techniques and wondering why your site isn't moving up the rankings after weeks and even months of hard work.

Chapter 8 – Social Media Strategies

Like, share, tweet, and plus one, the social networks' role in SEO has dramatically increased over the past several years. Google now pays close attention to just how many times a page is tweeted, shared, liked, or given a plus one. It's important to mix any good SEO strategy with a strong social media strategy, but knowing what to do and how to go about getting those precious social media votes can at times be difficult.

This section will give you some helpful tips on launching and managing an effective social media strategy to go along with your SEO campaign efforts and show you some insider techniques on getting more social media shares and votes than ever before.

Chapter 9 – Producing Results

Of course, like anything else in life, good things come to those who wait, and although this is not a personal development book, I can't help but highlight the importance of feeding your brain with positive input daily.

SEO takes work, and you'll find yourself at times putting in long hours trying to set things up properly. Fortunately, you have an SEO road map here for success; however, the road is long and hard and requires consistent effort on your part to produce lasting results.

It's easy to get discouraged at SEO as it is with anything else in life that takes real and consistent effort. However, if you can master the art of SEO, your ability to create instant and lasting wealth online will be unlimited.

There are few people who truly understand SEO and use it to their advantage. These few who follow through with SEO practices such as unique content creation, proper linking, social media campaigns, and everything else involved with SEO, are able to create significantly trafficked sites that ultimately enhance their bottom lines.

By understanding and having the knowledge to build and launch a site that will make it to the top of Google's rankings quickly, and stay there for a long time, is a skill that will pay off handsomely over time. Just imagine being able to find a domain, build a site with affiliate links and really good content, then work on driving that site to the top of Google's search results. The pay off - automatic income running 24 hours a day, 7 days a week, without rest. Sound enticing? Welcome to the world of SEO.

2
AGED DOMAINS

Known only to very few savvy Internet Marketers & SEO specialists, an aged domain is a domain that has previously been indexed by Google in the past two or more years. This is a requisite for the success of any SEO campaign since Google's algorithm has been beefed up to factor in how long ago a domain was first indexed by the search engine.

If you have a new, or relatively new domain name, Google's algorithm filters the impact of everything SEO related, On-Site and Off-Site, diminishing any optimization efforts you may try to institute in the first couple of years of a domain's existence. This means that links don't get as much weight, even if they are prominent ones, social media shares don't matter as much, even if there are many of them, and any other normally affective SEO effort's impact is dampened. As a result, the SEO score is diminished along with the visibility of that domain's listings on SERPs.

Being stuck with a domain that's new isn't the end of the world. However, if you're going to make any significant moves to rank higher on the SERPs, you must allocate an aged domain. An aged domain name is not considered aged based on the date of the initial registration of the domain itself (located in the WHOIS database), but rather, the initial date that Google indexed the domain.

An aged domain name can be either a domain name that you have owned for two or more years, or a domain name that was won at auction. No matter how old the domain however, if it was never actually indexed by Google, it's not considered an aged domain.

If you have a domain name that was registered and indexed by Google less than two years ago, and you're attempting to rank for highly competitive keywords, then your efforts will be nothing short of futile. In competing to rank at the top of Google's SERPs, you're better off purchasing an aged domain name at auction and building up the SEO value of that domain name, and linking your original domain name to the aged one.

Over time, your original domain name will increase in SEO value and won't have its results filtered (or Sandboxed) by Google. While this may be a difficult decision for some, without an aged domain name, you'll be trapped on low-level SERPs wondering to yourself how come you're not ranking high when you've done everything else to boost your site's SEO.

This is probably one of the most important insider trade secrets to SEO that's not discussed in many other places. Most people either gloss over this or simply haven't analyzed enough data and had enough experience with both aged and new domain names to be able to tell the difference. This one technique will not only save you time and frustration, it will help boost your bottom line in the long run.

GOOGLE'S SANDBOX

As children, we all played in the sandbox, but there's another little known virtual sandbox floating around in Cyberspace that many just aren't aware of. Google's sandbox, also referred to as the Sandbox Effect, is a method for filtering search results that decrease the impact of any link building, content creation and other SEO efforts that are implemented for new domain names. This results in the degradation of SERP rankings for any given keyword having high competition on an un-aged domain name.

You may be thinking that this is an unfair practice implemented by the search engine giant, however, many years ago, spammers would dominate the search ranking pages by buying up multiple varying domain names, duplicating content and creating link bombs with those keywords to the sites, rocketing them to the top quickly and easily. This has been very well documented in the past. To prevent this, and for other reasons, Google has created its Sandbox.

While the Sandbox Effect is something that has been

well documented in the SEO world, Google has never abjectly disclosed it or the exact set of rules that pertain to it. This is because the Sandbox has been put in place to prevent spammers and low quality content generators from dominating Google's ranking pages as they once did in the past, so it's pretty clear that Google most likely never will disclose all the details related to its rules.

You may have a domain name that you have been trying fiercely to rank on the first page of Google's search engine results, to your frustration, but have not been able to get it to budge after months of work possibly including content creation and heavy backlink building campaigns. In this instance, be aware that if the domain name is a new domain name, then your efforts are mostly going to waste. While there are special situations that may be exceptions to the Sandbox rule (such as obtaining a domain name with the exact phrase as your primary keyword), in most cases a new domain name will rank significantly lower than an aged domain.

Understanding what an aged domain name is and following along with some basic principles that are in effect when attempting to acquire an aged domain, is imperative to the success of your intended SEO campaign. Not referring to the date of initial registration of the domain itself (located in the WHOIS database), an aged domain refers to the first time that Google indexed its pages.

If a domain name was first registered in 2006 but it wasn't first indexed until 2012, the domain name isn't aged. However, if the domain was registered in 2006 and first indexed in 2006, then you have a well-aged domain name. This information is vital to the success of your SEO campaign, but finding the right aged domain name may be difficult so it will take some effort of consistently searching.

One other important issue to note here while discussing aged domain names and their acquisition is that you should not attempt to acquire an aged domain name that was in a completely different category or niche than the site that you intend to associate with it. The content should be somewhat similar to what you're attempting to rank for. For example, if you're trying to launch a children's toy ecommerce site, don't try to purchase a domain name that was indexed for skin care a few years back.

Although this isn't a major issue today, repurposing a domain name may become a red flag in the future, especially if you attempt to associate entirely different content with the domain than its historical indexes contained. Try to keep the niche or category somewhat similar to what it used to be in order to avoid any potential future headaches.

AVOIDING THE GOOGLE SANDBOX

You only have two choices if you're looking to avoid the Google Sandbox Effect: you can either wait until your domain has aged for two or more years, or you can purchase a domain name from an auction site or domain seller directly.

Even if you've already put considerable efforts behind an existing new domain name that you may have, purchasing an aged domain name will allow you to rank higher and faster than with a new domain. Registering an aged domain name will at least give you the opportunity to rank as high as the first position on Google's SERPs. Even with low competition for a given keyword, it's going to be very difficult, if not impossible, to rank a new domain name on the first page of Google's SERPs let alone be in the first position.

Of course, special circumstances could exist here, and if for example the new domain name is the exact same word or phrase as the intended keyword, there may be a chance to reach page one immediately. However, if there is heavy competition you will still see huge resistance even with a new domain name that meets this criterion.

Purchasing a domain name at auction doesn't require that much effort, and it's something that few know about or really take advantage of. I've found some of the best domain names that I own by combing through the auction sites on a periodic basis. These auction sites are not only dedicated to people willingly selling their domain names, they also house the crown jewels of domain names that have possibly unknowingly expired and are now available to scoop up, and those are recently expired domains.

There truly is no better way to get your content ranked quicker than by having an aged domain. Even if you do all the other things right, having a brand new domain name is going to sting for a long time. Google looks at a new domain name just like banks look at new businesses, as big risks. Whether it's the risk it will fail, produce spam, or whatever other reasoning it has, Google has instituted these safeguards and it's your job to ensure that you do whatever it takes to have the best fighting chance on ranking high.

By finding and purchasing an aged domain name, you will at least have the capability to rank your site high up on the SERPs, whereas with a new domain name, you will not. Simply put, new domains just aren't trusted by Google.

Cross-referencing historical Google indexed data is going to be critical during the hunt for aged domain names. By cross-referencing the domain data you will be determining whether or not this is an actual aged domain name that has been indexed in the past, or whether it's simply an old domain that sat dormant and never became a Website.

To conduct your cross-referencing work on the domain names you'll be using a Website called the Wayback Machine (http://archive.org/web/web.php). You can simply Google "Wayback Machine" to find it or enter in the URL. The Wayback Machine houses an archive of the Internet and its pages dating back to 1996. You'll need to use the Wayback Machine while searching for domains at auction so it's best to open it up in a separate browser window or tab while conducting your searches for an aged domain.

If you've ever tried to search for an aged domain, the process is relatively simple and purchasing an aged domain name is similar to purchasing a new domain name. The major difference is that the transfer usually takes a few days after purchase of an aged domain name as opposed to happening instantly for brand new, never before registered domains. But you know how the saying goes: good things come to those who wait.

The transfer period usually takes anywhere from 3 days to 6 days and sometimes happens before the expected final transfer date. Waiting a few days for an aged domain name is significantly better than having to wait a few years before you can rank a new domain on Google's SERPs.

USING GODADDY AUCTIONS

One of the Web's best resources for purchasing aged domains is GoDaddy Auctions. Not only do they provide domain names available by auction, but they also house domain names on the auction site that have recently expired.

Expired domain names are usually premium ones, going un-renewed for a multitude of reasons such as a re-billing credit card errors, no longer doing business, or an issue related to outdated email and contact information. These expired domains are gold mines possessing enormous amounts of SEO juice, so to speak.

To initiate the process of allocating a domain from GoDaddy Auctions, you can also simply point your browser to: http://auctions.godaddy.com.

When you arrive at the GoDaddy Auctions Website, you'll need to click on their advanced search hyperlink in order to access and adjust the filters that we'll require when searching for aged domains. The advanced search hyperlink is located where the arrow is pointing in Figure 2.1 depicting the GoDaddy Auctions Website homepage.

What we hope to achieve, by adjusting these filters, is to find a domain name that is in your niche and can fit the site you intend to launch or the existing business you're in. It's important to find a domain name that is at least in the same category because by using a domain name that was indexed for something completely different in the past you may encounter some resistance or even face de-indexing by Google in some extreme cases. This repurposing of the domain name must be done properly if you're going to succeed in your SEO efforts.

Figure 2.1 ~ GoDaddy Auctions Website Home Page

When sifting through the database of names that are available at GoDaddy Auctions, I would recommend setting the search filters as shown in Figure 2.2 (the highlighted sections display the recommended settings for searching). You'll be looking for a domain name with a minimum age of 5 years that contains a certain keyword related to your business, with a dot com extension that has a buy it now option.

If you're in the children's clothing business, you can use the keyword "clothing" but make sure that selector type is changed to "contains", otherwise it will look for an exact match and you can rest assured that clothing.com will not be available. The category has to make sense and it should match categorically with the present business that you're in to avoid raising any red flags in the future.

Take the time to look at some of the old Web pages in the Wayback Machine. archive to see what the past content of the domain was; see if it matches what you're intending on doing with it.

Figure 2.2 ~ GoDaddy Auctions Advanced Search Filters Screen

Upon successful initiation of a search on GoDaddy Auctions, you'll be presented with a number of domain results that you can review the details of by clicking on their respective rows. The most important component of this search isn't the actual age of the domain name, but the first time that the site was actually indexed by Google's search engine.

To determine if the domain was in fact indexed by Google in the past, after you conduct your search, launch another browser window or tab and navigate to the Wayback Machine (http://archive.org/web/web.php) and type in the domain names that you've located one by one. In the search results on the Wayback Machine, you'll either have data returned with history of the Webpages over time, as depicted in Figure 2.3 for Amazon.com, or a screen displaying that no historical index information is available.

Figure 2.3 ~ Wayback Machine Archive Search Results

Once you find the ideal domain name that has been indexed in the past within the search parameters specified, you should immediately purchase it before it's no longer available. Most people buying new domain names are not familiar with this technique on purchasing aged domains, and this one tip alone could put countless extra dollars in your pocket by being able to immediately sky rocket your site to page one or even position number one on Google search results within a very short period of time.

Without having an aged domain, you're looked at as the new kid on the block that doesn't get much attention for a while. Every effort that you take with a new domain name will be filtered by the Sandbox Effect and have less of an impact than if you were to use an aged domain name.

When you find the domain you're looking for, simply add it to your cart and continue through with the purchase process. After purchase, you'll be able to come back and check the status of the domain's transfer to see just how many days it's going to take (usually 3 to 6 day period from purchase to transfer).

Before purchasing the domain name it's critical that you ensure Google has previously indexed it. Check the Wayback machine's screenshots to confirm that the pages were actual Web pages and not just domain repository coming soon pages. The more activity and older the domain name, the better your chances are for ranking higher, faster.

3

KEYWORD RESEARCH

With billions of Web pages vying for search engine traffic, competing and clawing their way to the top of SERPs, picking and selecting the right keyword can either propel you high up on the rankings, or leave you sitting on the sidelines for a long time. SEO is a competitive field, but it's always possible to find some combination of words or phrases that will offer lower keyword competition while still fitting your product or service.

There are many tools that can be utilized on the Web in order to determine your probability of being able to rank on the first page of Google's SERPs. With 96% of clicks coming from that first page of Google SERPs, as opposed to the second page and beyond, it's no wonder why everyone is hard at work to position themselves on that jeweled first page. The more time that you spend doing the proper keyword research, the better your possibilities are going to be to rank at the top.

In the field of Internet Marketing, professionals who take the time to write a few well-researched articles each day with unique content are able to drive thousands of unique visitors to their blogs on a daily basis while earning themselves six and seven figure yearly salaries by promoting whatever product they choose to on those pages. Before they set about writing those articles, however, they invest their time into doing keyword research to ensure that they will be able to rank at the top quickly.

While you may not do this for a living, it's imperative to understand that spending the extra time doing quality research during the keyword phase is going to be time well spent.

BRAINSTORMING KEYWORDS

Your approach to the all-elusive hunt for the right keyword should always start with a brainstorming session. If you're a pen and paper kind of person, then you should grab a notepad in hand, and if you prefer the computer, then I would suggest opening up an Excel spreadsheet. Whatever tools you choose, pick one and immerse yourself in the hunt for the right keyword.

What you're going to be looking for is not only a primary keyword, but secondary keywords as well; this is applicable both for a site-wide search and an article-focused search. I can't express enough the importance of this phase, and time well spent hunting for the right keywords will be time well saved in the future when trying to rank on SERPs for those searches.

The first thing you'll need to begin with of course, is your niche. If you're looking to sell children's toys, cell phone accessories, weight loss products, or whatever it may be, try to analyze your industry and resultant keywords from different angles. Write down as many different ideas as you possibly can about your business, niche, industry, competitors, products, and customer demographics. This should be a good starting point for you when you start to actually analyze the amount of searches some of those terms gets compared with how competitive it is to rank for those keywords.

When brainstorming there are a few different approaches. There's a direct approach, say if you're selling a weight loss pill, you might simply begin with the terms "diet pills" or "weight loss pills". However, going beyond the direct approach to a specific type of product is an answer to a question such as "how to lose weight fast" or "best pills to take for fast weight loss". Now, you'll notice that some of these phrases are **long tail keywords** that offer one of the lowest barriers to entry in SEO ranking.

Long tail keywords usually have low competition but considerably good search volumes. When approached correctly, long tail keywords are one of the simplest types of search queries to rank first page or number one for, as you won't see as much competition for long tail keywords as you will for shorter keywords. An example of a long tail keyword would be "how to lose weight in less than 30 days" as opposed to just "how to lose weight".

When conducting your keyword research, keep in mind that you'll need to create unique content based around the keywords that you've selected. Now, if this is a site-wide keyword, then this may be a bit easier since site-wide keywords usually will not be long tail keywords. However, if you're trying to pick a keyword that wouldn't naturally appear in a sentence that often, then writing the content for it may pose a little bit more difficult for you.

Writing content for a short keyword is a lot easier than writing content for a long tail keyword, but it's harder to rank at the top of SERPs quicker. In retrospect, selecting a long tail keyword may make content writing more difficult, but the ease of ranking at the top of SERPs much better. Since factors come into play when ranking a keyword, you won't actually know how well you do until your content is out there and indexed. If you're just starting out, Google's spiders will be visiting your Website a lot less often, so you're force to wait longer periods of time until you can see a noticeable effect from the work you've put in.

The game of wait and see can be one of the most frustrating parts of the SEO business, but there's just no way around it. Until you have a Website with high page rank (4 or above) you won't see immediate results for ranking a keyword. You will have to wait at as much as 14 to 21 days to notice the initial effects of your SEO so it's important to do it right the first time around.

GOOGLE ADWORDS KEYWORD TOOL

The best method for researching the volume of search and competition for keywords is a tool provided by the search engine giant, Google, itself. The Google Keyword Tool, part of the Google Adwords suite, is a free online tool that can be used by anyone to do keyword research. The tool is very fast and effective and provides an enormous amount of insight into how rankable any given keyword is going to be.

To locate the Google Adwords tool, simple search the term "Keyword Tool" in Google and click on the first result titled "Keyword Tool – Google Adwords".

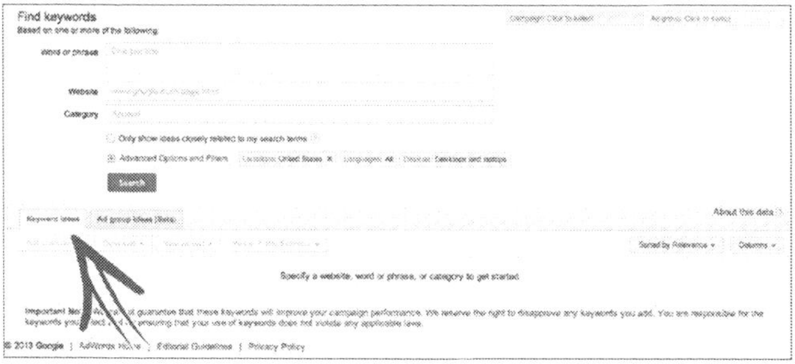

Figure 3.1 ~ Google Adwords Keyword Tool

Based on your keyword brainstorming session, you'll key in some keywords and enter them into the box entitled "Words or phrases". You can separate the words or phrases on separate lines, however, it's best to just keep it simple and start the search with your primary keyword or phrase from your keyword brainstorming session. For example, if your site has to do with heating repair in New York City, you may try to enter "Heating Repair Manhattan" or "Heating Repair NYC "as your keywords. Put yourself in the place of the person doing the search to try to visualize what you would type if you were searching for the product or service that you're trying to promote.

Try to stick with long tail keywords if you're marketing an article or blog post, and shorter, broader keywords, for site-wide SEO efforts. The ideal outcome of the research done using the Google Keyword Tool is to locate keywords that have high search volume and low competition. If your product is based on a specific locale and you're using the search tool from that locale, then you would focus on local search volume as opposed to global search volume.

The local monthly searches column is reflective of the

searches that are conducted from the area where your IP address is located. If you're logged in from Houston, Texas, than a search for "Heating Repair NYC" may not bring up enough monthly searches since most people from Houston, Texas won't care about heating repair companies located in New York City.

The two most important columns you'll be focusing on when conducting this research will be the "Competition" and the "Global Monthly Searches". You want to try to avoid any keyword that has high competition in the outset because it will be very difficult to rank high for them even with an aged domain. Your main target should be low and medium competition keywords that have a relatively high search volume.

The most ideal situation would be to find a keyword that has low competition with over 10,000 global monthly searches, or even more. Now this may be rare if you're targeting something broad, like Web design services, so be sure to analyze it from different angles by trying something like "Web design NYC" or "NYC SoHo Web Design Company". While the monthly search volume may be lower for this long tail keyword, your whole goal is going to be to rank at the top of the search. Showing up #1 for a keyword with 800 searches per month is much better than showing up on page 5 for a keyword with 100,000 searches per month.

Figure 3.2 ~ Google Keyword Tool Search Results Page

In Figure 3.2, you'll notice the results of a keyword search for the term "how to make money online" which not only returns back the results for that query, but underneath, some additional suggestions or similar searches as well. Each returned result has the volume of competition (high, medium or low), the global monthly searches and the local monthly searches. As stated earlier, you need to keep a keen eye open for low to medium competitive keywords with larger search volumes.

In the case of the search shown in Figure 3.2, the keyword search "make money online from home" would be a more optimal target than the keyword "how to make money online". With a search volume of 74,000 queries per month, the term "make money online from home" is one that would be a feasible target to gain first page and/or first position Google ranking for (considering that other requirements are met such as having an aged domain, unique well-researched content, proper On-Site and Off-Site SEO, and so on).

As your experience in conducting research on keywords expands, you will be able to quickly determine how easy or difficult it is going to be to rank at the top of a SERP for that search. Once you locate a primary keyword that you are going to target, be sure to locate three or four similar keywords by looking at the suggestions provided in the Google Keyword Tool search results. You'll be using these keywords to conduct additional research in the next section along with adding them in as page tags if you're using Wordpress.

SEO QUAKE PLUG-IN

After you've deselected all but Google, open up the SEO Quake Preferences menu, located in that same icon's drop-down menu (it's the first one at the top), click on Parameters and set the parameters for Google to: Google Page Rank, Google Links, SEMRush Links, SEMRush Linkdomain, Alexa Rank, Webarchive age, Twitter Tweets, Facebook Likes, and Google PlusOne.

Figure 3.3 ~ SEO Quake Icon on Firefox Browser

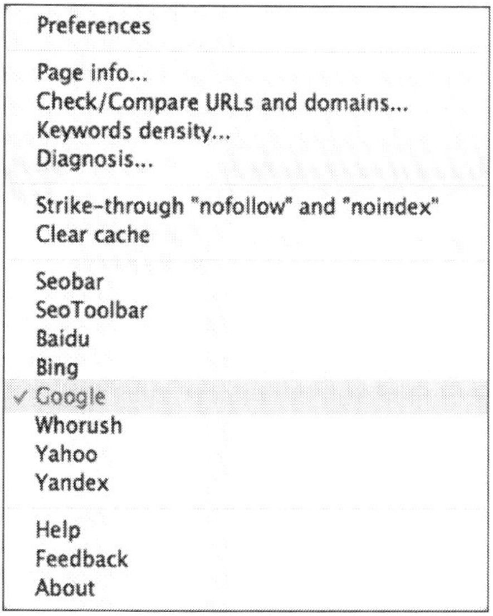

```
Preferences

Page info...
Check/Compare URLs and domains...
Keywords density...
Diagnosis...

Strike-through "nofollow" and "noindex"
Clear cache

Seobar
SeoToolbar
Baidu
Bing
✓ Google
Whorush
Yahoo
Yandex

Help
Feedback
About
```

Figure 3.4 ~ SEO Quake Only Google Search Selected

Once you have SEO Quake properly configured, you can start running some keyword searches with this newly installed tool. When conducting your searches you'll now notice that a small bar appears under each listing in the search. This bar provides you with crucial information allowing you to determine whether or not you will be able to successfully compete for the keyword tested.

Let's say for example, you want to rank at the top of Google's SERP for the keyword "Fly First Class Cheap" and you conduct a search on your browser with the newly installed plug-in or extension, SEO Quake. You'll notice as depicted in Figure 3.5, that each result now features an SEO Quake results bar just beneath it with detailed information based on the parameters that were selected in Figure 3.4.

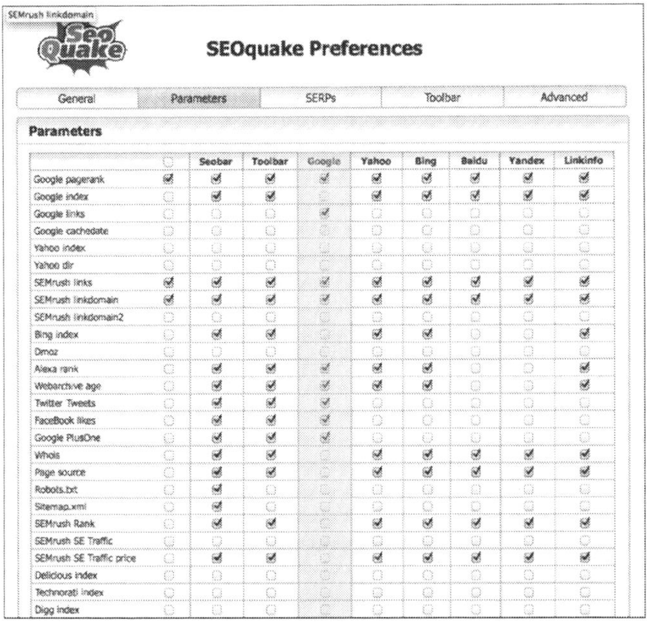

Figure 3.4 ~ SEO Quake Parameters

When performing a search like the one depicted in Figure 3.5, you'll notice several factors that either positively or negatively affect the SERP rankings of each listing. The first is the Alexa Web Ranking, shown just as "Rank" in the SEO Quake toolbars below each result. The lower the rank, the better the site is since Alexa quantifies the popularity of every single Website on the Internet, with #1 being the highest attainable number; having a rank higher than #1 would mean a lower popularity. Currently, the #1 spot is held by Google, with #2 and #3 spots held by Facebook and YouTube, respectively.

While browsing through the five results in Figure 3.5 and reviewing their Alexa rankings you'll notice that three of the sites are within the top 1000 most popular sites on the Internet, results #1, #3, and #5. Other important factors to take note of are links to the page indicated by the "L" with the Google logo next to it (there's also another "L" shown from SEMRush Links, another authority house on Website data). In addition to the Alexa Rank and the number of links you'll notice the domain's age, Facebook likes, Twitter Tweets and Google Plus Ones.

Figure 3.5 ~ Firefox Search with SEO Quake Plug-in
Installed

Looking at all the factors involved, we can see a very telling story from the data that's presented and be able to come to the conclusion that it will not be easy to rank for this keyword search. By doing a subsequent search for "fly first class cheap" using the Google Keyword you'll notice that the search term "fly first class cheap" has high competition and only 590 global searches per month.

Furthermore, in the search results depicted in Figure 3.5, all of the domain names are fairly aged. The oldest domain, in this case ranked #1 on this SERP, has the oldest age, dating back to January 25, 1999 while the youngest domain dates back to July of 2005.

How is it that the youngest domain name is ranked #2 in the results pictured in Figure 3.5? This is due to the fact that the youngest domain name has the most (135) links to that particular page while the other sites have 1, 0 or 8 links; in this case backlinks make up significant ground considering that the domain is far outweighed in age. This is an example of the power of backlinking (discussed in Chapter 7 on Off-Site SEO) and how it can propel you to the top spots on Google's SERPs.

Additionally, notice the social media statistics in the results on Figure 3.5; while it's unclear still just how much of a role they are playing in the overall rankings, you can be sure that they have an impact on rank. While it can be argued that Google may be weighing its Google Plus, as the highest-ranking factor in its algorithm since this is its own proprietary service, there certainly isn't any evidence to support that.

What is clear in Google rankings today is that social media links do matter. The specific weight of each network and its shares or likes are undisclosed by the search giant, but it's important to keep in mind that promoting on social media will be one of the key skills to develop in your overall SEO skillset. Getting enough people to click like, or share a post with any of the social media outlets can help in propelling you to the top of some SERPs.

In contrast to the "fly first class cheap" keyword option, if you look at some of the keyword suggestions further down the list in Figure 3.6, you'll notice that the term "business class vs first class" has low competition with 5,400 global searches done per month. In this instance, writing a well-researched article with unique content contrasting the positives and negatives of flying business class vs first class might be an excellent segway for launching into an article geared towards this specific keyword rather than the more difficult "fly first class cheap" keyword.

Let's say you're trying to target people looking to fly first class cheap, then maybe they can already afford business class, and you can use that article to discuss how you can secure tickets for first class for roughly the same price if not cheaper at times than with business class. This is just one example of piggy backing off of domain recommendations using the Google Keyword Tool.

Keyword	Competition	Global Monthly Searches	Local Monthly Searches
Search terms (1)			1 - 1 of 1
fly first class cheap	High	590	320
Keyword ideas (800)			1 - 50 of 800
flying first class	Medium	5,400	3,600
how to fly first class cheap	High	590	320
fly first class	Medium	6,600	2,900
how to fly first class	Medium	6,600	2,900
cheap first class tickets	High	12,100	6,600
fly first class for cheap	High	590	320
first class airfare	High	22,200	9,900
first class flying	Medium	5,400	3,600
first class airline tickets	High	12,100	6,600
business class vs first class	Low	5,400	3,600
how to fly first class for free	Medium	110	73
cheapest first class flights	High	14,800	4,400

Figure 3.6 ~ "Fly First Class Cheap" Google Keyword Tool Results

As you can see, by using a combination of information gathered from Google's Keyword Tool, along with information from SEO Quake, you can quickly put together a picture of just how easy or hard it's going to be to rank at the top of any SERP for any keyword. By looking at the domain's age at the top of the results, along with links and social media stats, its easy to determine just how easy of a task it will be to compete with these top 10 page one search results.

While the purpose of this is not to detract you from trying to compete, if you have a brand new site on a brand new domain name and you're unable to allocate an aged domain as described in Chapter 2, then you're going to find it very difficult to compete for keywords. However, if you do have an aged domain and you've done the proper research on the top 5 or top 10 results and you can see how many links each result has versus say their age and social media stats, you'll know pretty quickly for which searches you'll be able to achieve top rankings for.

SELECTING YOUR KEYWORDS

After you've done the research and narrowed down the options, you should select one primary keyword that will represent your page's primary theme or. In addition to your primary keyword it's good to select 4 to 6 secondary keywords or keyword variations that you can use to optimize your site and its pages.

Some of the general rules of thumb here are to not select any keywords that have less than 500 global searches per month, and don't select any keywords that have high competition unless you absolutely have to. If you're having difficulty locating keywords with lower competition in your niche, then try approaching the keyword searches from a different angle. For example, if you sell a specific kind of widget you may want to try searching for how that widget solves a need or a problem as opposed to the specific kind of widget itself.

You'll be using these main primary and secondary keywords on most of your non-article or blog pages so make sure that they fit your site and its niche as relevance factor is very important in SEO. Ensuring that keywords appear consistently in places like headings, titles, meta descriptions, image alt tags, and other important places will go a long way to site optimization in the long run.

Another thing to consider when selecting your keywords is to do searches for your competitors and see what they're using. You may want to run a few Google searches yourself for whatever product, service or industry that you're in. If your product or service is local, you may also want to try including some keywords with the locale and some without to see the effects it has on competition and search volumes.

4

ON-SITE SEO

Referring to work done by you to a Website or Webpage to bolster the effectiveness of its SEO, On-Site SEO plays a major role in your capability to rank in the top positions of searches. The ease of which you can impact your site by instituting effective On-Site SEO practices is far higher than those involving Off-Site SEO.

Having the ability to manipulate your page to match current SEO guidelines is simple enough when you know what to look for. However, when dealing with Off-Site SEO, it becomes more difficult to control external links, likes, shares, and tweets, how long they stick around for and any attributes associated with those links.

On-Site SEO involves the physical aspects of the design, setup, functionality and content of the Website itself. This includes the HTML & CSS code, keyword density, keyword styling, content, heading tags, internal linking, XML sitemaps, breadcrumbs, image alt tags, and any other relatable factors.

While as an SEO specialist you're not expected to be a

Website designer or programmer, having an understanding of the inner workings of how your site's underlying code functions and affects its appearance, and invariably its SEO, is highly recommended for anyone involved in the trade.

There are several resources available online that can provide you with a primer on HTML & CSS. From videos, to tutorials, online course, or blog posts, be sure that you at least have an understanding for the code even if you are not a programmer yourself.

If you're using a system like Wordpress for your Website, then your work will be much easier, but having the foundational knowledge of adjusting some configurations directly through the code itself never hurts, but in this case, it's not a requisite, just a recommendation.

There are several key factors to consider and address when it comes to On-Site SEO. Each and every time you add content (in the case of a blog), you'll be working with On-Site SEO so having the right tools & plug-ins if you're using Wordpress is going to be relatively important here.

When building your Website with Wordpress, plug-ins can really enhance and simplify your On-Site SEO work. They provide enhanced functionality to any Wordpress build that makes determining some of the variables much simpler such as the keyword density of a page. If you're not using Wordpress to manage your site, it's certainly something you should consider, as it will increase the ease with which you can conduct your day-to-day On-Site SEO efforts when creating content for your site.

There are two, primary On-Site SEO plug-ins I use with all of my Wordpress installations. Together, these two plug-ins, allow you to tackle virtually every On-Site SEO task needed to optimize your site. Not only do they help with page specific SEO but they also provide assistance with site-wide SEO as well.

The two Wordpress plug-ins that I utilize for On-Site SEO are the following (one is a free download, and the other is available by purchase only):

Wordpress SEO Plug-in – The SEO for Wordpress plug-in is one of the best free plug-ins that I've found for Wordpress, allowing you to update the meta description tag, title tag, and analyze other On-Page SEO data through the same interface you use to edit & post pages and articles. You can find this plug-in by Googling "Yoast SEO Plug-in."

SEOPressor Wordpress Plug-in – SEOPressor is another great plug-in for Wordpress that provides you with On-Site SEO scoring, with a complete breakdown of your SEO score factor (based out of 100). This is terrific if you want to take a lot of the guesswork out of your On-Site SEO. This plug-in is presently being used by over 125,000 Wordpress blogs online to manage over 15 million pages. You can find the SEOPressor plug-in by going to the following link: http://bit.ly/seopluginwp

Anytime you add a piece of content such as a Webpage or article post to your site, you'll be utilizing the same process for optimization. This process starts at the keyword research level, as discussed in Chapter 3, and continues through to both On-Site and Off-Site SEO. Once you have this process down, completing and fully optimizing each new page or post will become routine to you.

You'll need to ensure that you adhere to the rules and

guidelines laid out for you in Chapter 2 on Aged Domains. It's important that you have an aged domain name and conduct the proper keyword research in order to have a good foundation to build your On-Site SEO work on. Once you have your foundation in place, some technical details will need to be addressed as well. The overall HTML & CSS coding, keyword placement within pages and in relation to the Website fold are just some of the factors you will need to consider when doing your On-Site SEO work.

Google checks and analyzes data that's above and below the fold, and you want to make sure that you have certain important tags such as primary keyword headings for H1 and H2 above your fold. If you're using a system like Wordpress, then selecting a theme that is SEO friendly is important.

While you may not be a professional when it comes to selecting Wordpress themes, if you're looking to purchase a theme, read the descriptions and reviews carefully. Look for SEO optimized themes that place emphasis on not only an aesthetically appealing design, but also one that provides the highest possible optimized approach to SEO in its code. An excellent theme to use that's highly modifiable and optimized for SEO is the Blackbird Theme by InkThemes. You can find it online by going to the following link: http://bit.ly/inkthemeswp

While there may be a lot of little technical details to address when putting together your site, once it's complete your sole focus should be on creating unique well-researched content that you can then get linked, shared, and liked on as many networks and pages throughout the Web as possible.

SEO BLACK BOOK

WORDPRESS SEO PLUG-IN

Boasting over 3,300,000 downloads, Wordpress SEO is a free plug-in developed by SEO consultant firm Yoast that takes the capabilities of doing SEO with the Wordpress platform to a whole new level. While Wordpress has always been a strong foundational basis for SEO, adding this plug-in by Yoast allows you more flexibility over critical On-Site SEO elements like never before.

From the modification of page and post specific meta description fields, titles, and a robots.txt editor, the Wordpress SEO plug-in has an incredible array of tools to take your On-Site SEO efforts with Wordpress to the next level. If you're building on the Wordpress platform, having this plug-in is highly recommended to save time and improve your overall SEO efforts.

Installation for the plug-in is easy by navigating to the Plug-ins > Add New section of your Wordpress administration area. Use the keyword "Wordpress SEO" to locate the plug-in in the plug-in search and ensure that you install and activate it (see Figure 4.1). Once installed, you have the power of conducting nearly all of your On-Site SEO efforts directly through your Wordpress administration panel.

After installation, you'll have access to a settings screen that will allow you to modify some of the plug-in's system-wide general settings. Most of the default settings will work just fine, however, if you're interested in getting more technical you can access the settings as shown in Figure 4.2, and modify any of the information displayed. In the Dashboard, you can integrate Google, Bing and Yahoo Webmaster tools but if you've already verified your site with these tools then this is unnecessary.

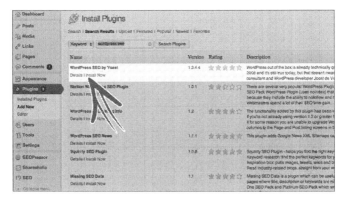

Figure 4.1 ~ Wordpress SEO Plug-in by Yoast Installation.

One of the most powerful aspects of utilizing a plug-in like Wordpress SEO by Yoast is the ability to change the meta description tag and title tag for each specific page and post. This is done directly through the same interface that allows you to add & edit pages and posts in the Wordpress administration interface, a capability that doesn't exist with the core Wordpress installation. Since Google weighs the meta description and title tags as factors in its scoring of your page for SEO, having the capability to modify these on a page and article specific level makes your SEO job that much easier and better.

While getting acclimated to this plug-in may take some time, the powerful features that it holds for your On-Site SEO work is well worth it. The company provides a guide on using the plug-in that is available on the company's own blog, which should answer most of your questions regarding its usage. You can find it online by going to the following link: http://yoast.com/articles/wordpress-seo/

Figure 4.2 ~ Wordpress SEO Plug-in Screen

Each time a new page or article is created, you can

utilize the built-in interface available directly on the add page or add article screen to optimize your page. As you add your content and save your draft, this plug-in will let you know if you've adhered to all the factors that derive an On-Site SEO score such as keyword in the title, content length, keyword in heading tags, keyword in page URL, keyword in content, keyword in meta description, and so on.

Wordpress SEO also provides a handy SEO check available in the right hand margin of your add / edit interface in your Wordpress admin. Indicating the level of completeness for your On-Site SEO, the colored circle changes from green, to orange, to yellow, to red, indicating just how optimized the page is with green being the best and red being the worst.

Figure 4.3 ~ Wordpress SEO Page Analysis

As you can see in 4.3, the Wordpress SEO plug-in provides the fields required for you to fully optimize your page or article with the title tag and meta description tag fields tailored for each post or page. Additionally, it can help you find related keywords for a primary keyword, as well as provide you with a quick scorecard to see how you're doing (indicated by the fields just below the Focus Keyword field).

For someone just starting up their On-Site SEO work, this truly does make it a no-brainer, however, just having the Wordpress SEO plug-in won't be enough to address all your On-Site SEO requirements.

SEOPRESSOR WORDPRESS PLUG-IN

SEOPressor is a unique plug-in available for the Wordpress platform, revolutionizing your On-Site SEO work. This plug-in assists with all of the various little factors that go into scoring a page for On-Site SEO effectiveness. Addressing this issue of fine-tuning that becomes complex to manage without an accurate system for tracking, SEOPressor is one of the most invaluable tools you will find in optimizing a Wordpress article or page.

Helping literally take the guesswork out of your On-Site SEO work, SEOPressor has sparked frenzy in the search engine optimization community, seeing over 125,000 installations over the past 3 years with over 15 million pages optimized. When used in combination with the Wordpress SEO plug-in by Yoast, it offers a fully complete suite of On-Site SEO tools for managing the optimization of site-wide SEO as well as page specific On-Site SEO for your Website.

While SEOPressor is a paid plug-in, it's by far one of

the best that you can find and will save you an enormous amount of headache when starting out with On-Site SEO. If you intend on doing multiple projects utilizing SEOPressor for Wordpress it's best to purchase the multi-site license as opposed to the single site license.

Installation of SEOPressor is simple and straightforward. Once the system is installed it keeps a score of your SEO for just your On-Site content (shown at the right hand side of the screen when add or updating pages and posts). While achieving a 100% score on every page & article you post is not required coming as close to 100% as possible is always good practice.

HTML & CSS SETUP

Whether you've hired a Web designer to build your Website, or you're doing it on your own, it's important that you have a clear understanding of what the best practices are when it comes to optimized HTML & CSS coding for search engines. Of course, if you're utilizing a Wordpress system, this will not be as important, but it's still good to have a foundational understanding of the code.

While a complete review of HTML & CSS is beyond the scope of this book, I will highlight some of the important elements of HTML & CSS as they pertain to On-Site SEO.

If you're not comfortable writing code or modifying existing code, then you should either hire a developer that you can work with on an ongoing basis from a site like Elance.com or Guru.com, or utilize Wordpress and get yourself a good theme you can use and make modifications to through the administration panel.

HTML & CSS have come a long way since the early days of Website development. In fact, early on developers didn't adopt CSS at all, and it really took time for the programming language to take footing in the industry. Additionally, in the past, it was not possible to completely design a site without the use of traditional tables, columns and rows, which created the foundational basis for early Website development coding.

CSS has enhanced the capability of designers and programmers to separate the Website layout code from the rest of the site, making it easier on search engines like Google to spider the Web and determine SEO related data much quicker.

Today, when laying out a site, the HTML & CSS setup is very important to search engine spiders, as they place heavy weight on where certain elements in your page's architecture appear. There's also heavy weight placed on an element's location to the Website's fold (where the Web page gets cut off by the standard browser and is forced to scroll down).

You want to ensure that your important keyword headings are placed above the fold if you are building the Website without the use of Wordpress. This would include the <H1> and <H2> tag for optimal On-Site SEO.

When working with HTML & CSS there are several practices that you (or your Web developer) should institute in order to successfully optimize your page for search engines to the greatest extent possible. Search engines really don't like to see a lot of code mixed in with text these days, which is why CSS is so important for separating your coding structure from the site text & content. Search engines expect a clean site with the proper elements addressed when it comes to On-Site SEO in order for you to compete at any level.

JavaScript should be avoided whenever possible within your page's HTML code unless absolutely necessary. A lot of what you can achieve with JavaScript can now be accomplished with HTML 5 & CSS so if you've hired a Web developer to assist you with your site, make sure that he or she is aware of this.

Keeping your Website's imagery to a minimum is also important. While we all want Websites that dazzle and look amazing, it's important to ensure that your site is using as much text within the design as possible. If you're utilizing a Wordpress theme, this is something that you usually don't have to worry about.

If you have a custom Website being designed for you, or you're having a theme modified, ensure that as many of the elements as possible utilize text as opposed to imagery. Years ago this wasn't as possible to make cross-browser and platform Website appearances look as similar as it is today.

The advancement of browser technologies, Website coding, and operating system fonts allow CSS coding to manipulate designs to look very similar across all browsers and platforms. You can virtually design an entire Website in CSS including gradations and other effects you could only achieve with imagery just a few short years ago.

META DATA

Meta data used to hold more importance than it does today. In fact, many of the meta fields are now obsolete, but there are however a few fields that still matter, and one important one that greatly still affects On-Site SEO is the meta description field.

Meta data is not visible to the human eye on the browser unless viewing the source code, and, first generation Website designers used to use meta data to propel their Websites to the top of search engines by instituting a now frowned upon Black-Hat SEO technique called keyword stuffing. Keyword stuffing would see the meta keywords literally stuffed full of similar keywords to the maximum character capacity in order to propel sites to the top of SERPs, and it used to work.

However, the days of keyword stuffing are now over, and meta keyword tags have lost all significance. Keywords are now obtained from the search engines through the usage of keyword density algorithms, weighing the keywords on the page based on the number of times they appear in relation to the total amount of words on the page, in addition to various other keyword styling factors as well.

The one meta tag that still holds relative importance today is the meta description field, which search engines use to establish a Website's description from. Although, even if the meta description field is not present, Google, and the other search engines will still spider the page to produce its own descriptions and display that upon serving up the search result.

KEYWORD DENSITY

Keyword density refers to the number of times your keyword appears on the page in relation to the total number of words. For example, if you have 500 words on your page and your keyword appears 10 times, then you have a keyword density of 2%. This is a very important factor when it comes to doing On-Site SEO.

Scouring the Internet, the search engines score and rank sites for their keyword density, keyword positioning, keyword headings, keyword styling, and keyword existence in title tags, amongst other On-Site data. During the creation of your content take note to focus on developing a keyword density of 2% to 5% in natural organic sounding manner. Oftentimes, when attempting to achieve optimal keyword densities individuals get so caught up that they allow the text to sound too "spammy".

If the written text does not sound natural, isn't well researched and well written, it will not rank high.

Dropping your keyword over and over again in an attempt to quickly wrap up your content creation tasks will allow it to sound forced and poorly written, and as a result get you demoted in the rankings.

No matter what you set about writing that's attached to the site you're working on, take the time in creating content that is well written, with keywords that are spaced well enough apart and sound natural and flowing and not forced.

Certain other rules should be followed and adhered to when composing your text, laden with keywords. A good rule of thumb is to ensure that your keyword appears once in the first sentence and once in the last sentence of your page's content. Space the rest of your keywords out periodically throughout the balance of the text, trying not to place too many keywords in any one single paragraph drastically more than the others.

If at all possible try to achieve a word length of at least 500 words for each page and post that you put out on the site. I've come to notice that content that's over 1000 words ranks even better, so if you're able to achieve this length of content for your page or article without making it sound drab or spammy, then I highly suggest you do this.

The distribution of your keyword, and the care that you take to write a well thought out, well-researched piece of content speaks volumes to Google and the other search engines indexing your site. Ultimately, not only does this bolster your SEO, it provides significant value to the reader of the content. By providing value, you're indicating that you're an authority, and by being an authority, your rank increases.

Having never written a piece of content, you may find some of this difficult at first, especially when attempting to distribute the keyword throughout the content without making it sound too forced. This will take some practice and getting used to and while you can outsource something like this, I highly recommend that you get acclimated to writing rich content with proper keyword distribution. It's an excellent skill to have no matter what type of marketing you set about doing in life.

If you're using Wordpress and you've installed the **SEOPressor Wordpress Plug-in**, scoring and keeping track of your On-Site SEO keyword density, amongst other things, will be simplified. This will make your job dramatically easier and take a lot of the guesswork out of On-Site SEO work that will have to be done on an ongoing basis to the site.

KEYWORD STYLING

Another On-Site SEO element influencing search algorithms is keyword styling. Keyword styling places a certain type of emphasis on the keyword, changing its appearance in the text to either bold, underlined, or italicized. Careful attention must be paid to placing this type of styling, or emphasis, on the primary keyword when building content for your page.

The guidelines on styling your keyword include having it appear in bold face font at least once (wrapped in <b></b> or <strong></strong> tags), in italicized font at least once (wrapped in <i></i> or <em></em> tags), and in underlined font at least once (wrapped in <u></u> tags) for every 500 words of content.

Ensuring that the keyword styling appears evenly spaced out throughout the content is good On-Site SEO practice. For example, if your content is 5 paragraphs long, place the bold keyword in the first paragraph, the italicized keyword in the third paragraph and the underlined keyword in the fifth paragraph.

While keyword styling can be done to your page's secondary keywords, it's best to stick with styling only for your primary keyword. Styling and optimizing a page for multiple keywords, while doable, is not recommended, especially if you're just starting out in SEO. You'll notice that the SEOPressor plug-in (version 5) does allow you to optimize for multiple keywords, however, in my opinion this will only serve to confuse search engines more than help you climb the rankings.

Simply focusing on your primary keyword for the page is an On-Site SEO best practice. Attempting On-Site SEO for multiple keywords, will only confuse the search engine spiders and you'll find yourself not ranking as well because of it.

Google uses a mixture of your keyword density, keyword styling, keyword positioning, keyword headings, title tags, and meta description tags to provide you with an On-Site SEO score. This algorithmic computation, coupled with other high level data it has about your site, allows the search giant to give your page a relevancy ranking that leads to your ultimate position on the SERPs. Trying to conduct On-Site SEO for more than one keyword will ruin your chances of optimizing to 100% of your On-Site SEO primary keyword.

Keyword styling, and other On-Site SEO requires finesse. It's easy to overdo it when it comes to keyword density and keyword styling. It's completely unnecessary to have your keyword be styled more times than required or have your keyword density be too high. The difficulty here is in having the page not look like it's been forced and written around your primary keyword. By doing so, you'll end up demoting your page if you don't end up adhering to some of these guidelines.

Try breaking up your page into sections, this way you

can use your headings to identify each section. For example, if your page is about the "100 Meter Dash", sections on the page can be diversified to use your keyword, "100 Meter Dash", in various form factors and ways. For example, types of sentences for this keyword may include those such as "History of the 100 Meter Dash" or "100 Meter Dash Fastest Runners".

If you're using a program like Wordpress to manage your site and you're working on a page layout or post layout, then you can easily use the built-in tools to highlight and modify (or style) your text. This is a lot simpler than coding in direct HTML and having to place the tags, save your file, then upload it via FTP each time, which can become fairly tedious and time intensive after a while. Save yourself some headache and utilize a Wordpress installation even if you're already a Web developer or seasoned Web designer.

USING HEADINGS

In HTML and CSS wrapping text with heading tags creates headings that are both stylized aesthetically and also weighted for On-Site SEO. Headings not only alter the appearance of text making it look a certain size, color, and font family, but headings are also used by search engines to gather an understanding of what the page is about.

By analyzing heading tags such as the H1, H2, and H3 tags, Google, and other search engines, can estimate what the page or article is primarily geared towards when combined with the other On-Site SEO factors. For this reason, it's important to have your primary keyword appear in all these heading tags, but not to over do it.

An example of using headings would be to wrap a title such as "How to Lose Weight" in an <H1> opening tag and an </H1> closing tag. In HTML the forward slash in the tag denotes that the tag is closing and the tag lacking the forward slash is the opening tag.

In our example, this would look like this in HTML: <H1>How to Lose Weight</H1>. Of course, if you're using Wordpress this can simply be achieved by highlighting the text and changing the styling from "paragraph" to "heading 1" or switching to "text" or "HTML" mode and placing the tags in manually.

There are six different headings in HTML that can be stylized with CSS but only the first three have real weight. The <H1>, <H2>, and <H3> tags are given special importance by Google and it's important that they not only appear in your HTML or Wordpress article, but that each of these tags contains your page's primary keyword.

INTERNAL LINKS & BREADCRUMBS

Internal links & breadcrumbs are an important part of On-Site SEO as they help the search engine spiders to find other pages on your site. Building internal links on your Website will allow you to spread the link juice around the site and provide easy access to the search engine spiders to quickly index your entire site.

You should have a clear and easily navigable overall Website structure setup with proper menu bar and internal links within your content to other pages on your Website. When linking to internal content, try to utilize the keyword that the target page is using for SEO, as this will properly marry the destination page with the keyword.

Breadcrumbs are a type of navigational linking structure that help the search engine spiders, and human visitors, to quickly jump through sections of a site. For example, when you're shopping for a laptop on an electronic Website you may see a breadcrumb link structure that looks something like this: Home > Electronics > Computers > Laptops. A structure like this makes it very easy to navigate through a site no matter what page you may be located on.

Internal links and breadcrumbs are very important when it comes to On-Site SEO as they denote a clear and identifiable site structure (similar to a site map). Without internal links, pages of content may be completely lost to search engine spiders and may never be seen by human visitors.

When utilizing a Wordpress theme, linking & breadcrumb navigation become no brainers, as most themes will support this type of linking structure. As commonplace as it may be today, some sites and developers are still not instituting proper linking & breadcrumb structures so it's important for you to be aware if you're having a professional develop your site for you.

IMAGE ALT TAGS

Image alternative tags, or alt tags, are tags, or attributes, added to an HTML image that provides the search engines with an alternative text reference to your image. Usage of the image alt tag dates back to the early days of the Internet, and today, the alt tags are still important for SEO since search engine algorithms will use the presence of your page's primary keyword in the alt tag in their relevancy scoring.

On each page, whatever the primary keyword is, you should have an image alt tag that contains that primary keyword. Going a step above and beyond this is to actually name the primary image as the primary keyword using hyphens to separate the words. For example, if your page's primary keyword is "How to Cook Eggs Benedict" then you should name your main image located on the page as how-to-cook-eggs-benedict.jpg or whatever image file extension suits your image.

The image HTML version optimized for On-Site SEO would look similar to this:

<img src=http://www.yourdomain.com/images/how-to-cook-eggs-benedict.jpg" border="0" width="585" height="300" alt="How to Cook Eggs Benedict">

As you can see in the example above, the image alt tag is the primary keyword for the page and the image has been named as the primary keyword of the page. This is the most optimal way of having your image files on your page optimized for SEO. If you're utilizing the Wordpress system for your Website, setting an image alt tag is simple upon upload and can be defined during the process of adding that image to your page.

ON-SITE SEO CHECKLIST

The whole purpose of On-Site SEO is to address all the factors on the page that affect your SEO score. As discussed in the sections of this chapter preceding this one, there are a multitude of elements to address in On-Site SEO when building a site or page.

To make matters easier, using the combination of Wordpress plug-ins will enhance the ease with which you can simply and effectively address all of these elements through the same interface with which you add or edit the actual Webpages or article posts.

Below is a checklist of items that should be addressed to achieve optimal On-Site SEO. The same elements, aside from the first one in the list, will be available to you through the two plug-ins directly on the page or article that you will posting through Wordpress. Ensure that you adhere to these as closely as possible to ensure excellent On-Site SEO.

- ☐ CSS separated from content
- ☐ Keyword in title tag
- ☐ Meta tag description uses keyword
- ☐ Keyword in H1 tag
- ☐ Keyword in H2 tag
- ☐ Keyword in H3 tag
- ☐ Keyword in bold tag
- ☐ Keyword in italics tag
- ☐ Keyword in underlined tag
- ☐ Image alt tag utilizing keyword
- ☐ One image on page is named with keyword
- ☐ At least 500 words of content
- ☐ 2% to 5% keyword density
- ☐ Keyword in first sentence
- ☐ Keyword in last sentence
- ☐ At least one internal link within content
- ☐ Usage of breadcrumbs

OVER-OPTIMIZATION WARNING

With the release of the Google Panda & the Google Penguin, Google has become very particular with sites that are attempting to over-optimize their content. If your content does not sound natural and it looks like your keywords are too forced, you will not rise in the rankings, and risk being demoted for those particular search keywords.

When you are writing your content, keep it very natural sounding. You do not have to use your keyword in the exact search term in each section. You can do variations from time to time, which will in fact help you rank higher. This is called LSI, or Latent Semantic Indexing. LSI is a technology used by Google to determine similar words and phrasing for search terms, so don't beat yourself up trying to force your keyword term in each area. Keep it as natural sounding as possible for the best results.

5

ANALYTICS & TRACKING

Every marketer knows that he or she needs some sort of tool of measurement to determine whether or not they're achieving the marketing results that they're after, and SEO is no different. Without the capability to track and analyze your traffic, you will be unable to determine whether or not your efforts are in vain or if they're paying off.

There are a couple of really good tracking tools that can be implemented when tracking a site's Website traffic. One of the most well known tools comes from Google itself, and is called Google Analytics. Utilizing Google Analytics does require you to setup and create an account with Google, so if you already have an account, just navigate your way to Google Analytics in order to access this system.

Getting setup with Google Analytics is relatively easy and straightforward and you can add any number of Websites & profiles into your Google Analytics account for tracking. A recent addition that Google has added has been the real-time tracking tool that now allows you to view the traffic to your Website in real-time as opposed to only static data that used to have a long delay.

To this day Google Analytics is still free, however, that may of course change in the future, but it's doubtful considering that most people allow the sharing of their Website data with Google which only helps to improve their search engine algorithm's knowledge that much more. With this knowledge Google can determine data sets that it couldn't gather before such as how long a user stays on the site, what other pages are visited, and so on. This is all valuable knowledge that Google can then use to improve it's own search results. For example, if a site has a page that captivates users' attention spans for minutes on end say with a video, Google may just increase the SERP ranking of that page due to its "stickiness".

Once you have Google Analytics setup, you can follow the instructions provided by the search engine giant to integrate the code into the header of your Website for tracking. If you're using Wordpress, then installing the **Google Analyticator Wordpress Plug-in** is probably the easiest way to get up and live with your analytics right away. When linking the two it will prompt you for access, then allow you to choose which analytics domain you would like to link to (if you have multiple domains that is) and the integration is fairly easy and straight forward.

Aside from Google Analytics there's also other alternatives as well for Website analytics. One of the most popular alternatives is a PHP script called Piwik available as a free download. You'll need to ensure that you're on a Linux Server, or if you have a Windows Server, that you've installed PHP as a Fast CGI add on. This can get rather technical if you're on a Windows server, and if you have a hosted solution it won't work at all on Windows since you won't be able to modify major components of the server such as making PHP available in IIS (the Windows Server

Platform).

Whichever analytics platform you select, the importance of being able to determine your Website's traffic is paramount to understanding how well your SEO efforts are paying off. Not only will you be able to determine the demographic location of your visitors, you'll also be able to determine just how they found you (whether through keyword search, a referral link, or direct entry) and what pages they visited on your site and how long they stayed there for.

Of course there's a wealth of knowledge to be found from analyzing Website statistics but the basics are relatively simple and straightforward and will allow you to determine the success rates of your SEO campaigns. The important information you're looking for are number of visitors, how they got to your site (whether through referral link or organic search), and what keywords were used to reach your site. Obviously when you're optimizing for specific keywords you want to ensure that people are finding your site through those keywords so this would be the type and style of information to look for in your Website's analytics.

One important detail to note about using Google Analytics is that due to privacy concerns, Google won't give you full details about your Website's visitors. For example, if you're trying to determine how many people from New York City typed in a specific keyword to get to your site you won't be able to do so since Google does not log the IP addresses for you to view.

Furthermore, you may notice that on some Google Analytics results you receive a "not provided" in place of keywords used. The "not provided" is attributed to Google's secure search results, extending even more privacy to its users and less information for you to analyze.

However, your ability to analyze content viewed on your site will always be available to you, but beyond that if you're looking to be able to determine all the minute details of your Website's visitors, you might want to opt to install Piwik instead of Google Analytics.

TRACKING YOUR PROGRESS

Once you've setup and installed your analytics program of choice, it's important that you get very acclimated with the program and its various different reporting statistics. It goes without saying that tracking and analyzing your Website's traffic once you've begun conducting SEO work is imperative.

Understanding what to track is of real importance in gauging the success of your promotional efforts. Unfortunately, SEO is a hurry-up-and-wait type of undertaking. The changes that you make now may not be reflected in search results for days or even weeks to come. For this reason, understanding what to do and how to do it right the first time is important if you're going to be at all efficient with your time.

Clearly we're trying to understand the effectiveness of specific keyword searches and our ranking position in each of those searches. One thing you need to understand first is that Google's search results are localized so if you're searching for some keyword from one location, you may receive different SERP results than if you search from another. This affects what you see, and what someone else sees in another, city, state, and country.

While it's important to understand that SERP rankings are localized, there are various tools that you can use to track the average result of your organic search listings for your keywords. One such piece of software that's amongst the most popular is called SEOMoz. By tracking your keyword placement over time, you'll determine whether or not your SEO efforts are paying off and make adjustments when necessary.

6
CONTENT IS KING

SEO is such a multi-faceted industry that weaves together so many different complex little elements, that it's no wonder many people truly never get a handle on mastering the profession. Being a so-called "SEO Guru" takes a lot of time and experience and making plenty of mistakes. I can't tell you how many times I've messed things up just trying to get it right.

There are so many errors that you can end up making simply because you don't know any better at the time. These can be costly, causing you to lose ranking fast, and some mistakes just cannot be undone when the damage has already been done. Risky behavior taken while trying to quickly rank for a keyword can end up backfiring and demoting you on the SERPs so proceed with caution. If you're still not clear about something go back and reference it or do a search online to get more specific information.

When it comes to tried and true top rankings on Google, while all the other factors are important, content is and always will be king. If Google and the other search engines recognize that you have unique well-researched content you hold an extremely good chance of ranking well. Unique content on an aged domain is like having a concrete foundation for a house that spans as deep as one for a skyscraper.

Of course, meeting all the other On-Site SEO parameters required for a high scoring page is crucial. All other things being equal however, your excellent content will propel you to the top.

Your ability to write excellent content will set you apart from the others competing and clawing their way to the top of SERPs. Learn to write excellent content while doing everything else required of you in SEO, and you will the ranking game over and over again.

The best way to get really good at content is to write every single day. Practice writing everyday in order to improve your writing skills, whether it's online or offline, it's important that you continuously engage in writing to build up this skillset.

If you don't presently have a blog, then get one and use it to post on a daily basis. Setup a blog that addresses a specific niche, do keyword research, and write well-researched articles with unique content that help to provide value to people's lives.

Whether you want to just write for fun just to get better at it, or you're looking to monetize your blogging career, writing daily will help you to incredibly improve this skill. By running Google AdSense ads on your blog, or promoting affiliate programs through Clickbank or Commission Junction, you can easily monetize your blog to earn money while also improving your SEO abilities.

Practice makes perfect. Writing and blogging daily will force you to be able to formulate your thoughts and ideas much more clearly over time. If you're able to build a blog with any formidable amount of traffic, then you will learn how to create the winning formula for boosting SEO for yourself or a client. If you've followed along with all of the other suggestions I've offered up until now, you will get very good at SEO and ranking just about anything if you institute these practices on your blog or domain name.

It is wise to throw up a cautionary notification here to inform you that if you're doing SEO for the first time around, it's utterly imperative that you be very careful and cautious. While performing a task that may be seemingly routine such as pinging Google with links that house your keyword and domain (Chapter 7), you could get yourself into hot water by overdoing it. What may excite you at the time as an opportunity to quickly climb the rankings may be construed by Google as a Black-Hat SEO technique, and get you demoted very quickly, so be careful.

It may even be advantageous for you to register an entirely new aged domain name and start from scratch, setting up a blog and practicing ranking that domain name for a keyword and niche. While the process may seem somewhat tedious in the beginning, by practicing care and doing SEO with caution your traffic will climb slowly and steadily until one day you explode onto the top of SERPs.

When setting up your own blog on an aged domain, you can choose any topic you wish to write about. Find a niche that you enjoy or a hobby that you're fond of and find your aged domain in that category, ensuring that your intended new content matches the name or the historical indexed content of that domain. This process will help you get really good at researching keywords, producing content and ranking for whatever it is that you may choose to rank for.

Always begin by using the Google Keyword Tool and SEO Quake plug-in or extension to analyze the competition on the first page for any keyword. By consistently doing keyword research, and creating well researched, well written articles that provide valuable information, you'll be surprised just how much Web traffic you can create.

When you set out to write your content make sure you spend a good amount of time researching the area and topic that you'll be writing about. You'll be surprised to find out just how much additional information you can uncover about a topic that you might already think you know everything about. Don't ever be too overconfident because you can always learn more, do more and provide more value when writing so make sure to give it your best effort each and every time.

SELECTING A TOPIC

When building and developing content for your site you should always follow the overall theme of the site and not steer too far off into other areas of interest. If you have a product review site, for example, then stick to writing product reviews and not spending time writing articles on off-topic subjects.

By focusing your content building efforts on a specific niche, you effectively boost the SEO juice of the entire site as you add more information related to that niche and promote each piece of content on its own. By doing this, the cumulative SEO value of your site increases since these pieces of content are all tied together through tag or category links.

Writing may be difficult for you in the beginning, especially if you're trying to come up with various ideas to blog about. While it can be tricky acclimating yourself to this, it's another skillset that you will develop by practicing it on a daily basis. The better you get at this, the more chance of success you will have in SEO and ranking high.

To combat article and Website writer's block, there are several good methods you can use to come up with new ideas for your content. The first is by using Google's News Alert for your niche. If there's a company that's doing very well or a top producer in your niche, then setup a Google News Alert for that.

No matter what niche you're in, there's always a company, brand or individual sparking frenzies of search queries conducted each day for more information on them. These work well to provide you with up-to-the-minute alerts on relatable news that you can read, digest, then reorganize and redistribute on your own site or blog.

Of course, it goes without saying that your content must be 100% unique, and by practicing to read news-related information from various sources and put together your own short articles, you'll get very good at writing copy and content that is unique and well researched.

Besides for creating Google News alerts, other ways for finding fresh content to write about are to ask questions about your topic or industry and see if you can answer those questions. Use the six question types of Who, What, When, Where, How and Why and pose them at a company in your niche, the economic condition, competition, or any other relatable topic you can come up with. Brainstorm and get creative, then get busy writing and practicing every single day.

WRITING YOUR CONTENT

Nobody likes dull, difficult to read content, but when writing your content it's easy to allow yourself to let it get drab or to run on. Furthermore, writing content for a Website from an SEO angle can get tricky, and can come across sounding spammy in an effort to attain a high keyword density.

When writing your content remember to keep in mind that you're going to want to hit at least a 2% keyword density, approximately. If you go under a little that's okay, but try to keep it at around a minimum of 2%. You'll also want to ensure that your keyword appears in the first and last sentence of your content as well as evenly distributed throughout the rest of the text and not just bombarded into one section. However, doing all this while achieving content that also sounds good and flows is tricky, but it's the ideal goal.

If you're having difficulty placing your keyword within

the body of your content, don't force it. You can find other creative ways to place your keyword in the content, for example if you're doing an article on how to ride a bike, you could use subtitles with the keyword and the step number before each step in the process.

However, it's important not to overdo this as well. Having your keyword appear too often in heading tags can also hinder you as opposed to help you. Just remember to keep in mind the rule of moderation; try not to overdo anything because when it comes to SEO slow and steady wins the race.

Try planning out your content prior to writing it and keep in mind that you're going to want to have a minimum of 500 words per page or article and optimally 1000 words or more. The longer the article, the better it will rank on SERPs and concentrating on hitting 1000 words for each article or page of content is important if you're going to have any chance of vying with other listings for competitive keywords.

Before you set out to write your content, be sure that you do the proper keyword research. Of course, you'll have the primary keyword for your Website, but considering that you'll be building content for your entire site, for each section, make sure that you do the keyword research, select a primary keyword along with secondary keywords for each page and article. Gear your content towards these keywords and follow the rules laid out in Chapter 4 On-Site SEO Optimization for the best results.

7

OFF-SITE SEO

Off-Site SEO (also known as Off-Page SEO) refers to all the SEO work done away from your Website that help it rank on SERPs. Link building, social media marketing, forum posting, and blog commenting, are all examples of Off-Site SEO work.

The primary goal for your Off-Site SEO efforts is to build up as many high quality, IP address diverse, and keyword diverse links back to your site possible. The linking must look completely natural and organic for you to rank high. If Google sees 10,000 backlinks with the same keyword over and over created in a very short period of time, it will know you are participating in "link schemes", considered to be a Black-Hat SEO technique and your site will be demoted, or further Sandboxed (if it's new) on the SERPs.

Off-Site SEO is an enormous undertaking. With so many changes being instituted recently by Google it seems as though at times you're walking on a tightrope trying to balance all the different tasks required while not violating any algorithm rules in place. It's not enough to just have an aged domain, unique content, good keyword density, and near perfect On-Site SEO. You have to tell the search engines that you're relevant by creating a diverse set of links bridging back to your Website.

If you think of your Website when you first launch, it's likened to a lonely little island sitting off the coast of millions of other islands and continents ranging from very small to super-sized. These surrounding landmasses are other Websites that have varying different page ranks.

The page rank of a Website ranges from 0 to 10 and can be determined by downloading and installing the Alexa toolbar (available on all browsers except safari). The Alexa toolbar is another tool that you'll need in your arsenal of SEO weapons to wage the war in climbing to the top of SERPs. While this may sound a little bit outlandish, SEO is no walk in the park, and Off-Site SEO is going to be the bulk of your work, so be prepared to dig in and "grind".

Virtual link bridges spanning the unending divide of Cyberspace, connect your Website with the rest of the Internet world. An island with no bridges is an island with no traffic, but an island with many bridges to and from other islands has the opportunity for an exceedingly large amount of traffic. Since link relationships have a very early root in search engine rankings, these link bridges play a major role in relevancy for search results.

Not just a determination of the number of links back to your Website, your ranking is also based on the popularity of those links. For example one link from a very popular site like Facebook or YouTube (both have page ranks of 9 out of 10) has much more value than 10 links from very unpopular Websites with low page ranks.

The goal in Off-Site SEO is to build up as many links

as possible from as diverse of a range of Websites as possible. This link building will take up a majority of your Off-Site SEO efforts.

While link building is a critical component of Off-Site SEO, too much link building in too short of a time can actually hurt you. When Google released one of its recent algorithm updates called the Google Penguin, in April of 2012, one of its sole goals was to seek out Websites that were participating in these so-called "link schemes".

If it determined that a certain site went from virtually no links, to thousands of links in a very short period of time, Google's Penguin algorithm came to the conclusion that the site was participating in "link schemes". This is also part of what we call the Google Sandbox Effect that can happen not only by having a new domain name, as discussed in Chapter 3, but also by participating in these link schemes.

It's important to not only have a good quantity of links that are from high quality sites and to have link diversification, but also that the links built up to your site have diversified keywords and are created gradually and not dramatically. This may be a lot of rules to remember, but just keep in mind that you always want your efforts to be as organic looking as possible.

Having 1,000 links created in a period of one week all with the same two or three keywords is very unnatural, even if you those links are coming from very different Websites. The key here is to have a very diversified set of keywords that includes your primary keyword, secondary keywords, and generic keywords. Once these links are created, they must be pinged slowly through a drip feed system, like the one available through Linklicious.

While you may not understand it now, anytime you

have an obsession over something and you track it on an hourly and daily basis (like some do in the SEO industry), you come to know what works and what doesn't over time and you can see major shifts clearly when they occur. It's like watching a stock on the stock market move up and down with its fluctuations as it ebbs and flows both against and with the market.

There are always factors that can be attributed to the rise and fall of a stock, and the same goes for the rise and fall of a domain name on the SERPs. The difficulty here is to be able to determine what works and what doesn't in a timely fashion in order to make adjustments geared around ranking you higher.

The issues with SEO at times are that changes may not be noticeable for two or more weeks from the date you publish a piece of content and begin conducting SEO work on it. Unless you have a very popular site that's heavily trafficked (PR 4 and above), any changes you make may take considerable time to show up as an improvement on the SERPs.

SEARCH RELEVANCY

The purpose of the search engines' searches are to provide its users with relevant search results that will come as close to possible in providing answers to the questions they are seeking. Staying relevant is paramount if you're going to get noticed and rank at the top of SERPs by Google and the other search engines.

By striving to provide more and more relevant search results as the Internet becomes more crowded, Google has been forced to fine tune its algorithm many times over by rewarding those that stick to the rules, and punishing those who try to bend them.

When building your Off-Site SEO campaign, your goal should always be to look as natural and organic as possible. Google loves natural looking links that point to unique well-researched content, so use that information to your advantage by building content that is useful and unique. This foundational element of the search giant's computations has always existed and will most likely increase as time goes on.

When conducting Off-Site SEO efforts it's easy to try to rush through theses processes simply because you feel pressed for time or want to achieve immediate results. However, the more time you take and effort you put into building a solid Off-Site and On-Site SEO foundation, the better the rewards will be. Consistently creating unique well-researched content with natural and organic looking links should always be your primary concern.

You might have come across people or companies promising #1 Google rankings that are guaranteed based on some special arrangement they have with Google. Albeit, there are no companies that have special arrangements with Google for ranking #1 on searches, and this would be completely counter-intuitive to the relevancy culture that Google has tried so hard to promote and preserve.

No one can possibly guarantee you a first position ranking on Google. So many factors come into play, as we've discussed in this book, that guaranteeing a #1 position on the SERPs is just not possible unless you're Google itself.

The best-proven results will come to people who follow the rules and apply these principles consistently over a period of 60 to 90 days and beyond. Trying to rush these efforts by bending the rules or cheating with Black-Hat SEO techniques will ultimately lead to your ranking demise.

Another important point to note in our discussion about backlinking is that your competition on searches holds valuable clues into the eyes of search engine relevancy for a keyword. In Chapter 3, I discussed strategies for keyword research and utilizing the various tools available to you to see how the competition is ranking the way they do. I discussed using SEO Quake alongside the Google Keyword Tool to be able to estimate your ability to rank on the first page for any given search result. These are very valuable tools in judging how well you will be able to rank for your keywords so embrace them and use them often.

The more relevant your overall page is to the keyword being searched, the more likely you'll rank at the top. For example, it will be difficult to rank an investment article high on a blog that has its primary topic of discussion as celebrity news. Of course there are some exceptions to the rule such as just how popular that site housing the article is, but for the most part, try to ensure that your keyword is relevant to your site-wide topic or niche.

Over time, as you work on SEO for specific pages and boost each page respectively, it will help the collective group increase in SERP rankings. Since these pages will most likely share tags or categories that create a linked relationship between them, this will result in the collective rise of the domain's search engine visibility along with its pages and articles as well.

BACKLINKING

Backlinking is one of the largest undertakings that you'll be involved in when engaged in the practice of daily SEO. Backlinks are an essential part of any SEO campaign and it's a major weighing factor in the overall search engine algorithm that ranks your site's importance and relevancy.

Backlinks are like little bridges created from different landmasses to your new Website and when Google first started out, it started with the underlying theory that the number of backlinks created rankings. The more backlinks you had the more important your site was. Of course that has morphed significantly with the addition of many of the factors that I've covered in this book, but backlinks still remains as one of the core principles to placement on SERPs.

So, you're probably wondering to yourself how many

backlinks you're going to need in order to rank your Website high up on the SERPs. Well, there really isn't any clear answer to that and it's going to fluctuate based on your competition. As I discussed in Chapter 3 Keyword Research, it's important to understand the competition in order to be able to "snipe" your way to the top of Google. This is going to be done by using tools such as the SEO Quake plug-in and the Google Keyword Tool along with any other keyword analysis tool you may decide to invest in during your SEO career.

While understanding your competition and the number of backlinks that they have is important, you should set your sights on building as many high quality, diversified backlinks on a consistent basis as possible. The backlinks will need to be drip-fed to Google in a manner that seems organic and not as though you are paying to build these links or participating in a "link scheme".

There are a few important guidelines when it comes to backlinking that you should keep in mind. Not only are there different page ranks where a backlink can come from, there are also different types of backlinking structures that can be built. While the magnitude of backlinks is important, it's also important to understand that the "link juice" coming from a Website with a high page rank such as YouTube will be much higher than several backlinks coming from lower page rank sites (such as forum comments, blog posts, etc.). Aiming towards quality as opposed to quantity will get you much further in boosting link juice for your site.

Creating backlinks from popular social media profile pages is one excellent way to begin your link building campaign. Sites like Facebook, Twitter, and Google Plus are excellent starting points for any such efforts. Begin with your profile pages on the big three social media sites, and continue on to setting up profiles and dropping your site's link on authority sites as well.

An authority site is a site that anyone can post on such as YouTube, Squidoo.com, HubPages.com, Scribd.com, and others. Start with profile pages from each of the authority sites, making sure that a backlink exists to the site that you're working on. If it's a site for a client, then make sure that the client places backlinks in each of his or her profiles on these sites or create the profiles for them. Where possible, create the backlinks with the primary keyword of the site (this can be done on a site like Google Plus and a few select others).

While manually creating backlinks is a lot of work, there is software available that provides for automation such as SEnuke XCr SEO, and XRumer, but unless you're well versed in these it may be a better idea to outsource your backlinking work to start with. You can also use an online service such as DripFeedLinks.co or OneHourBackLinks.com for a very organic approach to link building on your own terms.

POST-PENGUIN BACKLINKING STRATEGY

As discussed earlier, Google has released various different algorithm changes over the past several years. The search giant is constantly shaping and transforming its algorithm to be smarter and better, forcing those working on ranking sites to try to stay one step ahead in order to maintain relevancy.

One of the more well known recent algorithm changes by Google has been the Google Penguin update. Google Penguin, an update to the algorithm that was first announced by Google in April of 2012, aimed at punishing and demoting sites on SERPs that participated in any SEO practices that violated Google's Webmaster Guidelines. This included things like keyword stuffing, cloaking pages, building mass amounts of links or purchasing paid links, and duplicating content. Websites that were ranking high who employed these practices got a severe demotion in ranking as a product of this algorithm change.

With the release of the Google Penguin, the search giant essentially sent a loud and clear message to the Internet as a whole informing them that while working to increase a site's ranking is okay, it won't tolerate those that try to bend and break the rules. This has forced SEO specialists to create Post Penguin practices that won't violate the search engines rules; it's made everyone a little bit more honest in the SEO world.

This is all very important when it comes to performing backlinking work for whatever site you may be trying to increase the SERP presences for. Google is looking for sites that not only have unique content, and lots of links, but also links that are diverse and organic. Just think about finding links to a site say in a forum or a blog post, that link isn't always linked with the exact same 4 or 5 keywords each time. To appear more organic, your link building activities must include some generic terms such as "click here", "learn more" or "get more info" beyond just the primary and secondary keyword links.

The essential set of rules for backlinking then, in the current Google algorithm environment are:

High PR Links – Every good Off-Site SEO backlinking strategy must provide backlinks from high PR domains. Try to space out these links over time and not build them all at once, as it will appear less organic if you do so. These high PR links will come from profile pages and once the profile page has been created, a good practice would be to ping them with a service like Linklicious.me. Concentrate on building four or five high PR backlinks per week from profile pages on popular social media and authority sites.

To create high PR backlinks you can use the following Websites:

Facebook.com

Twitter.com

Plus.Google.com

Folkd.com

Stumbleupon.com

Pintrest.com

Zootool.com

Springpad.com

Oneview.com

Diigo.com

Delicious.com

Reddit.com

Blinklist.com

Keyword Links – Linking with your primary keyword is important in order to create that relational bond between your Website and your keyword, one that Google will recognize and index. Take your primary keyword along with three or four secondary keywords (based on your keyword research discussed in Chapter 3), combined with 4 or 5 generic keywords and begin creating backlinks, link pyramids and link wheels by either purchasing them from a site like Fiverr.com, DripFeedLinks.co, or OneHourBackLinks.com.

Link IP Diversification – Google likes to see as much of an IP diversification as possible from sites that are housing your links. This means that the links should not all be located on the same site, but spread out on sites all across the Internet. You can achieve this by purchasing your links through proven vendors who provide diverse link building programs. Once these links are created however, you'll need to ping them in a manner that looks organic by drip feeding about 40 to 100 links in per day through a program like Linklicious.me.

Web 2.0 Links – The Web 2.0 links of the past may not have the same meaning as they do in the present day. Web 2.0 links refer to sites that offer more interactivity beyond just the standard static data display. This could mean an interactive forum or other community online that has some page rank.

EDU and GOV links – To further the diversification needs of Google's algorithm, the EDU and GOV domain names have special importance to the search engine. Google weighs these domain names a little bit differently and provides a little bit more importance to them than regular domain names of equal PR value. Getting EDU and GOV links are very good for your link diversification.

Social Media – Of course, there's the all important social media links back to your content. Links and shares from sites like Facebook, Twitter, and Google Plus are gaining more and more prominence in the eyes of the search giant. Beyond just sharing the links on your own, Google's algorithm will put more weight on a page or site that has multiple shares or likes by different people. Google knows that this type of activity is unique to real human beings or real human accounts actually vouching for a page or site so having a diverse amount of shares, re-tweets, and plus ones is important.

As you can see, the work of an SEO specialist in the link-building Off-Site SEO field is immense. Creating a diverse and organic looking backlinking structure is going to be something that you'll need to work on and plan prior to diving in. You will get demoted in the SERPs if you create lots of links in a very small period of time and ping them all at once.

To appear organic you must create the links and ping them in a way that looks natural with keywords that look natural. This is very important to the success of your site. Furthermore, to give your site more link juice, you should be linking to different pages in the site other than just your home page. By linking to other pages, you're telling Google that not only is the home page important, but so is the rest of the site.

BUILDING LINK PYRAMIDS

You may or may not have heard of the term link pyramid in the past, but these are powerful linking structures, that until just recently, were one of the primary tools that one could use to sky rocket a site to the top of SERPs. After the release of the Google Penguin, however, link pyramids, while still effective, can also backfire if Google flags it as a "link scheme".

A link pyramid is a pyramid of links consisting of three or four tiers with the top tier being considered the "money page". The money page would be your Website, article, email capture page, or any other page that you're attempting to get ranked at the top of SERPs.

The bottom few tiers of links will consist of links that link from the lower level to the level just above it only. The lowest tier of the link pyramid would be the lowest page rank links – these may be PR0 or PR1 links from blog comments, forum posts, obscure foreign profile pages or any other low page rank site pages.

The bottom level would link to the links in the level just above it, which would be higher-ranking links such as PR2 to PR4 links. Subsequently, those links would lead up to the tier above it, say Web 2.0 and social media links, all of which would lead to the top of the pyramid, the money page.

Building effective link pyramids takes a bit of finesse. You can't have it be perceived by Google that you're trying to quickly clamor your way to the top of SERPs so you must build them delicately. What I mean by this is after you've purchased your link pyramid from a vendor (such as off of Fiverr or another similar site) you'll have to slowly drip feed the links by pinging only a small amount to Google each day. This way, the link pyramid looks more natural and not forced. The link pyramid should also be built with a mixture of your site's real primary keyword and secondary keywords, along with generic keywords.

Pinging can be done in multiple ways through multiple software programs; however, there are a few online that are fairly reliable and affordable. You can ping up to 2,500 links per day for free through a site called Linklicious.me and also set a drip feed (i.e. 40 links per day) to feed through to Google for pinging, making it look more natural.

You can also take advantage of a site like DripFeedLinks.co to build your own link pyramid as well, rather than purchasing it from a vendor off sites like Fiverr. Although Fiverr is a great resource, for those that like to do things on your own DripFeedLinks.co is a terrific resource for building your own organic looking links and link pyramids.

BUILDING LINK WHEELS

Link wheels are another powerful SEO tool, and when used properly, and in conjunction with other link building methods, can propel a site high up on the SERPs. Link wheels refer to a network of sites all of which link to the next site in the wheel. For example, if we had five sites, A through E, A would link to B, B to C, C to D, D to E, then E back to A. All of these five sites would also link to the main site or "money page". The links to the money page in the link wheel are like the spokes on a wheel with the five sites being the actual wheel surrounding the center.

Link wheels are another tactic that Google has attempted to squash with the release of the Google Penguin, however, this has been something that has proven to be more powerful of a linking structure. The most powerful kinds of link wheels are social media link wheels where your social media profiles are all connected to your site and also to each other through content sharing. As you can imagine, this is a very powerful link wheel since social media sites have very high page ranks and much of the linking done through here seems more organic. Creating your link wheel with social media sites that all have connected profiles is a powerful form of a link wheel.

Link wheels, if done improperly can have a negative impact on your site's link juice. By creating "lazy link wheels" a site can actually get penalized and have all of the link juice reverted if a spoke is removed on a link wheel for spam. This happens, for example, when content is posted that looks "spun" or is not original. Some blog platforms are even deleting blog posts from profiles that only have one blog posted with more than 2 outbound links, so there are many things to take into consideration when trying to create these types of linking structures.

Today, however, you have to think outside of the box in order to propel yourself to the top of the SERPs. Not only do you need to create a powerful link wheel, but also having a combination of all linking methods is the most powerful and effective way that you'll move up the SERP rankings and stay at the top.

OUTSOURCING

It's difficult for most individuals engaging in SEO work on a full time basis to tackle all there is to do that's involved with it, let alone someone who has a primary job working elsewhere. SEO is difficult, there's no question about that, and the most difficult part revolves around the creation and distribution of unique content that's well researched. Without this primary building block it's very difficult to get search engines to rank you at the top of SERPs.

If you've never written before, and you find it difficult to come up with unique content, you do have the option of outsourcing your work to other individuals. While finding and locating an individual or business that can provide you with quality content at a reasonable price may be difficult, they do exist out there.

When you're at the stage where you feel you'll need to outsource some of your work, there are several resources online that you can turn to. From article writing, to link building there's an endless stream of providers ready and willing to help you with your SEO needs. Once you understand the basics of what SEO entails and have some experience under your belt, you can budget your time and finances on different aspects of the project. But when it comes to article writing, there really is no better person for the job than yourself.

A lot of what happens during the Off-Site SEO process can be outsourced but if you're outsourcing your content creation you have to ensure that you find a company or an individual who can deliver good unique content that has been properly researched. There are several sites on the Internet where you can search for outsourcing your content creation efforts such as on Elance.com, or Guru.com. These sites are dedicated to helping bring buyers and sellers of all sorts of projects together.

Another terrific resource for outsourcing that I've found major success with is Fiverr.com. The concept behind the site is that sellers sell you any type of product or service that costs a minimum of $5 (with optional add-ons for the more advanced sellers). Fiverr.com is a great place to outsource link-building efforts, since there are many sellers willing to do both manual and automatic link building for your site from just $5.

Fiverr.com has one of the best resources of cost-effective sellers for SEO services. To locate them simply navigate your browser to Fiverr.com, click on the "Online Marketing" tab on the blue menu off to the right, navigate to SEO, then sort by "Rating". In the list, you'll see a large number of sellers with various different SEO services to offer. You can also search Fiverr.com for any of the following terms: "link pyramid", "link wheel", "backlinks" and then sort by "Rating" to find the best sellers offering these types of services.

Figure 7.1 ~ Fiverr.com for SEO Outsourcing

Figure 7.1 displays the options to select on Fiverr.com in order to find top-rated SEO services. One suggestion here is that you try to vary your usage of sellers on the site (don't buy all your links from the same seller). Each SEO service here is a little bit unique, some are more organically linked, some have low PR sites, some have high PR sites, some are link pyramids, some are link wheels, and so on. If you vary up the SEO services that you purchase, you'll be sure to provide a wide enough variety of links to make Google happy.

One thing to keep in mind that you'll need to look out for on Fiverr.com when searching for vendors that offer link pyramids, link wheels, or direct links that are mostly Dofollow and try to avoid any that offer a large amount of Nofollow links.

When researching vendors on Fiverr be sure to read the reviews and see what negative reviews, if any, a vendor has. It's best to also communicate with a vendor before hand too if you have questions about a particular vendor's services as they're always willing to help provide you with further information.

Additionally, look for vendors on Fiverr that will not ping the links for you before delivery and if they do, that they do so with an optimal drip feed rate. It's best to communicate this with them prior to placing your order in order to be clear because some vendors on Fiverr will ping all your links for you at once, essentially creating link juice suicide.

While some of these concepts may be foreign to you and difficult to understand at first, just keep the underlying principles of natural and organic always in the back of your mind when conducing any Off-Site SEO work. If it can't be considered natural and organic, don't engage in it as you risk major demotion on the SERPs if you do so.

LINK QUALITY WARNING

Anytime that you outsource, or purchase a mass amount of links, you run the risk of getting flagged by Google for participating in "link schemes." If you don't know what you're doing, you could end up damaging your Website as opposed to helping it. Proceed with caution, and only purchase links from reliable sources and make sure that they are quality links. Do the research because in this Post-Panda and Post-Penguin Google search world, you risk penalization anytime you aggressively tackle SEO.

Of course the best strategy here is doing all natural links, but if you don't have time for that then look to using Websites like Fiverr.com, OneHourBackLinks.com, DripFeedLinks.co with caution. Do your due diligence before running head on into anything.

PINGING

It's not enough that you have to go out and create this complex and vast array of backlinks that link back to your Website, but in order to get Google to crawl and find them you have to do something called pinging. Since the majority of the sites that you'll be obtaining backlinks from will have low page ranks or no page ranks, Google may never actually crawl those pages.

It's estimated that Google only crawls about 5% of the Web that houses low page rank or no page rank sites. Without any directive to go index a page with a low or no page rank, Google spiders may never end up visiting it and your hard work in creating those links will go to waste, since they will never get indexed.

Pinging is a task that you're going to need to get used to doing each time you create an array of links back to your site. There are two different types of pinging services that you'll be using here. The first is a pinging service for your page's URLs that you create and build over time. This type of pinging will essentially instruct Google to visit the page on a periodic basis that you've established such as every 3 to 10 days.

Each time you post a Web page or article, you need to ensure that it gets pinged on a regular basis by using a service like Pingler.com, which will ping Google spiders to visit any link on a periodic basis (from every 3 days to every 10 days). If you have content that gets updated regularly you should set this to every 3 days, and if it's less often you can pick any other day up to and between 10 days.

In addition to ensuring that your own content gets pinged, you'll also need to ensure that any mass amounts of backlinks that are created are pinged as well. To do this you can utilize a service like Linklicious.me that will allow you to drip feed link pings of up to 2,500 per day (free account), use their basic account with 10,000 links per day (paid account), or you can opt for their pro account giving you 50,000 links per day (paid account).

Pinging is very important, since your grueling efforts of creating these backlinks takes time, you want to ensure it's time well spent because without pinging those links they may never get discovered and your site will never get credit for those backlinks.

The goal with pinging mass amounts of backlinks is that you want to make this appear as organic as possible to Google so you shouldn't be pinging thousands of backlinks per day. You should use the drip feed system of pinging to drip about 40 to 100 links per day to Google's spiders per domain or page that you're working on. Doing this will make your link building appear much more organic and your ability to climb the SERP rankings that much greater.

R.L. ADAMS

8
SOCIAL MEDIA STRATEGIES

With the explosive growth of social media networks like Facebook, Twitter & Google Plus, social media has not only become an important component of our lives, it has also become critical to the success of any SEO campaign. We use social media everyday to connect with the people we love and care about, and watch people's lives play out on the screen in front of us. For some, social media plays such an important role in their lives that nearly everything they do is documented from either their home computer or mobile device.

Google has of course taken notice of this explosive growth, not only by launching its own social media platform called Google Plus, but also now by beginning to give weight to social media likes, shares, and tweets more than ever before. While the weight that Google gives for each share on various different social networks is unknown, it is clear that it is providing more prominence for pages & sites that have heavy shares through the social media realm.

If you haven't already done so then it's important to setup a Facebook Page, Twitter Account, and Google Plus account for whatever person, product, or service that you're promoting in order to start garnering page likes and shares through the social media world. If you're unable to do this and you're working for a client, then this is one of the directives that you must give them as this is going to play a very important part in your SEO work since one important task in your Off-Site SEO efforts is to garner as many likes, shares, re-tweets, and plus one's as you possibly can.

Social media shares are important because they come from real human people clicking on a link saying that they either liked something or wanted to share it with the rest of the world. Getting someone to like or share a page sometimes isn't that easy, especially if it involves a bland or dry topic. It's become increasingly important to get people to share and like your content, whatever it may be, due to the impact these very powerful high page rank backlinks have in terms of Off-Site SEO link juice.

Of course most people already have a Facebook account and Twitter account, but if you're one of the few that doesn't' have these, then it's important to get this setup right away. Besides for these two social networks, having a Google Plus account is critical now as well.

There are hundreds of social media platforms out there today that have taken the term Web 2.0 to a whole new level, and Google is starting to take notice. It's also become increasingly clear by the high page ranks of some of these sites, just how popular they have become. When managing an effective SEO campaign one of the hats you are going to have to wear will be the Social Media hats.

While managing sharing content through 3 sites may sound overwhelming, try doing it on dozens of sites at a time. There are ways, however, that you can automate some of this work. Of course, this would become virtually impossible to manage after a while, especially if you're tackling several projects at once. For this, reason, it's important to engage in content syndication, discussed in the following section, which will ease some of the workload here.

CONTENT SYNDICATION

One of the best, most effective strategies that you can use to begin syndication of your content on social media networks is to use the power of the tribe. Whenever working and collaborating with others in this field (and other marketing fields), group efforts always trump individual efforts. You know how the saying goes, "there's no i in team", and it certainly holds true here.

Going about syndicating your content is difficult without the power of a tribe and automatic content syndication platforms. Tribepro.com provides an excellent syndication platform for sharing your content amongst hundreds, if not thousands of people in your tribe. The system offers its members a unique platform to be able to quickly syndicate content and build up heavy high page ranking backlinks almost instantaneously.

Tribepro.com requires a membership fee and also requires that you have a subscription to Onlywire.com, a service that provides the actual syndication pipeline used by Tribepro.com. While this can get moderately costly, it's probably one of the best investments that you can make in the SEO industry, allowing you to quickly and effectively build very high page rank backlinks to your content through a simple interface.

Content syndication can also be placed on autopilot with Tribepro.com. By adding your RSS feed to the site, it will automatically feed your content into the tribe on a daily basis. This is a terrific hands-free approach to doing a major part of your SEO tasks.

Of course, merely just doing content syndication is not enough, but when coupled with the strategies discussed in Chapter 7 for Off-Site SEO, can tremendously grow your SERP presence quickly and effectively.

9
PRODUCING RESULTS

The SEO business is a complex one, forcing you to weave together various labor-intensive Web-based marketing efforts to produce a single end result. Of course in life, nothing worthwhile would come easy, and the same saying goes for SEO and the industry as a whole. Wrapping your head around Google and its fickle algorithm seems overwhelming at first, but as you verse yourself in the industry it will make more and more sense over time.

A resounding theme in Google's algorithm changes boils down to just one thing: how relevant and important is your content. Google wants to produce the most relevant search result to the searcher, and doesn't like it when it finds people try to fool it into ranking something higher than it should be.

If you step back to look at Google and its present algorithm, you'll notice just how much its changed and evolved and gotten smarter. Gone are the times when you could spend a few days building mass amounts of links, stuffing keywords into meta tags, and exploding your

Website to #1 in the rankings. Today, the Google algorithm is extremely smart and intuitive, and getting to the top of any worthwhile SERPs requires effort, real and consistent effort.

If you've had any brush-ins with Google SEO prior to diving into this book then you know just how complicated it can be to compete for some keywords. At times, it feels like you're driving against a brick wall while producing absolutely no results, but this is by design. Google makes it intentionally difficult to climb the rankings on SERPs because it doesn't want to give away those jeweled top spots to just anyone. It wants those top spots to go to those most relevant listing, and to be relevant you need to have been around for a while, be properly linked, and have good unique content with excellent On-Site SEO.

It's easy to get discouraged when you're dealing with search engine rankings. Sometimes it seems as though you do all the right things with no changes in sight, especially when you're monitoring those results on a daily and even hourly basis. When you follow the steps in this book, and practice a little bit of patience, you will experience dramatic, results and improvements over time.

Normally when doing SEO work, I tell my clients to expect the most results after the 90-day mark. Of course, a lot can be done prior to that 90-day mark, especially if you're dealing with a non-competitive keyword. However, for the most part, the clients that I've worked with all want to get to the top of competitive keyword SERPs, and to do that requires sincere effort along with a good amount of time for full indexing to occur.

Here's a look back at a summary of what Google is looking for in its ideal page one SERP listings, and what you should be aiming to achieve in your SEO work.

How old is the content – As discussed in Chapter 2, Google wants to know if the domain is aged and has some history. If not, you're going to have some difficulties in achieving high rankings. Another thing Google is looking for is how new the actual piece of content or page you're ranking for is. While older content will still rank, Google does like to find new fresh content for topics that are age sensitive such as news related topics. Make sure that you keep the content fresh but have an aged and well-indexed domain for optimal SERP results.

Is the content easy to read & navigate – Is the content easy to read and navigate? If your content isn't pleasing to the eye, then it isn't pleasing to Google. Trying things like making the text a similar color to the background to hide keywords, having all of your heading tags below the fold, or attempting to cloak pages will get you demoted on the SERPs. Try to keep your site looking clean with separated HTML & CSS code and keep most of the important content above the fold.

Is the content unique & well researched – Google's algorithm is smart, and can determine how well a piece of content is written and sounds. Whatever mathematical equation they've come up with, it works to filter out the junk and spam out there, so make sure that whatever you write and place on your Website is unique, well-researched and not duplicate to anything else on the Web. You can use a resource like Copyscape.com to check for duplicate content.

<u>How relevant is the content to the search query</u> –
Relevancy is the largest factor in search engine results, so
you'll want to ensure that your content is relevant to the
search keyword that you're targeting and that you've
instituted all the proper On-Site SEO guidelines suggested.
Simply put, don't try to write about something far off topic
from your keywords, as this is considered a Black-Hat
SEO technique and will get you barred from climbing to
the top of SERP results for any given domain.

<u>Does the content have enough organic links</u> – Google
and the other search engines love well-linked content as
it's telling them that this content is important enough to
have people link to it. Of course, the way you go about
producing those links will take some finesse and pushing
too hard too fast can get you flagged by the search engine
for participating in so-called "link schemes". Try to keep
your linking organic looking and institute some patience
while drip feeding a reasonable amount of links per day
and not flooding the search engine with thousands of links
at a time. It's easy to get over excited when you have a list
of 10,000 links ready to be pinged that point to your site,
but flooding this many links will surely hinder you more
than help you.

FEEDING YOUR BRAIN WITH POSITIVITY

In life it's easy to get discouraged with whatever it is that we set out to do. The reason why there's so many fad diets and get rich quick schemes out there is because human beings have something call shiny object syndrome; we like to participate in the newest and best product or service but never really make it beyond just a couple of weeks.

Your goal is to stay committed and not give up, over time, you'll see lasting results, but anyone that promises you immediate Google #1 listing results or says they have a special arrangement with the search giant, is fabricating the truth. No one can guarantee you the #1 spot on Google, and Google doesn't place any special search conditions on its advertisers' organic search results either. The Google search engine's purpose is to show relevant organic search results, period.

There's several ways to get severely set back in the

SEO industry so make sure this doesn't happen to you. If you try to participate in any Black-Hat SEO techniques your site is going to fall so far off the search rankings that it may be difficult for it to ever really recover. Make everything that you do look organic with your Off-Site link building efforts. Great ways for Off-Site SEO link building include participating in sites Tribepro.com where everyone syndicates each other's content on their own real social networks, this is powerful stuff.

It's also important to stress that when building your keywords, if you're setting about purchasing keywords from a site like Fiverr, make sure that you have a mixture of 30% generic keywords to 70% real keywords. So, for example, if I'm linking to a site and using 10 total keywords then seven of those would be real keywords that would include my site's primary keyword, and three of them would be generic keywords. The generic keywords should change for each page you link to, so you can use "click here", "learn more", "get details" for one set of purchases then change it up for another.

It's important to assess where you are each day when it comes to your SEO efforts and ensure that you come up with your own daily action plan that you'll execute everyday to improve your SERP rankings and site's overall SEO standings. These could include things like daily affirmations, self education on YouTube, reading motivational or inspirational material, reading other blogs about SEO or your niche to get ideas for unique content, and so on.

Whatever strategy or plan of attack you come up with, stick to, never giving up until you reach your goals.

OTHER BOOKS BY THIS AUTHOR

If you enjoyed this book on SEO, I would really appreciate it if you could take a few moments and share your thoughts by posting a review on Amazon. You can post a review by visiting the following link - http://www.amazon.com/dp/B00B7GIVSE

I put a lot of care into the books that I write and I hope that this care and sincerity come across in my writing because in the end I write to bring value to other people's lives. I hope that this book has brought some value to your life. I truly do.

Also, feel free to also take a look at some of the other books that I have available on Amazon. The following titles can also be found that I have authored:

SEO Simplified – Learn Search Engine Optimization Strategies and Principles for Beginners - http://www.amazon.com/dp/B00BN7PGEY

SEO White Book – The Organic Guide to Google Search Engine Optimization - http://www.amazon.com/dp/B00BUOPFHI

How Not to Give Up – A Motivational & Inspirational Guide to Goal Setting and Achieving your Dreams - http://www.amazon.com/dp/B00BSB02KI

Kindle Self Publishing Gold – Unlocking the Secrets of How to Make Money Online with Kindle eBooks - http://www.amazon.com/dp/B00BQJB5QM

Kindle Marketing Ninja Guide – Killer Marketing Strategies for Kindle Book Marketing Success - http://www.amazon.com/dp/B00BLR40FC

I wish you all the best in your SEO educational pursuits.

All the Best,

R.L. Adams

APPENDIX
SEO TERMINOLOGY

Aged Domains – An aged domain is a domain that has been in indexed by Google at least two or more years ago and it's a critical component of any successful SEO campaign. Google penalizes new domain names, making it very difficult to rank any keywords at the #1 position or even on the first page of search results for that matter in the beginning. Purchasing or having an aged domain will be one of the critical factors in your success for ranking a site high for any given keyword.

ALT tags – Also known as alternative tags, these are the tags that appear within the HTML <img> tags that present the alternate data to the search engines to provide a description of what the image is. For optimal search engine rankings you should have at least one image ALT tag that correlates with your site or page's primary keyword.

Backlinking – Likely to be your biggest undertaking when it comes to SEO, backlinking is the effort involved with creating hyperlinks that link back to your Website. There are several rules involved in backlinking that are covered within the content of this book in Chapter 7 on Off-Site SEO.

Black-Hat SEO – Black-Hat SEO is a term used to describe a SEO tactics that are not compliant with Google's Webmaster Guidelines. Black-Hat SEO techniques are frowned upon by the search engine industry. Examples of Black-Hat SEO techniques are trying to hide keywords within HTML comment tags or trying to cloak pages.

Breadcrumb – A navigational aid used on Websites, breadcrumbs not only allow users to quickly jump through informational sections on the site, they also provide high SEO value by allowing the search engine spiders access to quickly navigate and spider through a site, indexing data faster and more efficiently.

Cloaking – This is a technique that delivers different content to the search engine spiders than it does to real human visitors. The cloaking technique is oftentimes used to mask the real content or change the real content of a page and make it appear differently to a search engine spider. This is considered a Black-Hat SEO technique and while it is sometimes used for legitimate purposes, it is oftentimes used to display pornographic material to real human visitors while only displaying non-pornographic material to a search engine spider.

CPC – Cost-per-click, or CPC, is a term used in online paid advertising to indicate click through percentages. The cost per click is calculated by diving the number of clicks with the total amount spent on the advertisement. For example, if you spent $100 on an ad and 200 clicks was received; the CPC would be $0.50 cents.

CSS – Cascading Style Sheets, also known as CSS, is a style sheet presentation markup language that is used to position elements, layouts, colors, fonts, images, and construct a Web page on the whole. While CSS is used primarily in styling HTML Web pages, it is also used to style XML and other documents.

Dofollow Links – Dofollow links are an attribute associated with an HTML hyperlink that tell a search engine to continue to link through to the site, disseminating some of the site's important link juice. These are very powerful types of links that work well when pointed to your site or to a link pyramid that leads to your site. When a search engine sees a Dofollow link they continue linking through to the site, passing part of the SEO link juice that would have been offered to that page had the link been a Nofollow link.

Duplicate Content – In the search engine world, content is king, but duplicate content is the court jester. Copying large chunks of content to your site is one of the biggest no-no's in the industry. The search engines will figure it out sooner or later and you will be demoted in the rankings. If you're going to do SEO right, make sure all the content is high-quality and unique content that's well researched.

Headings – HTML headings are blocks of code that are placed around certain words, styling and providing a certain level of prominence in the overall page structure. Heading tags range from <h1> through <h6>, however, in the modern SEO world the first three hold the most importance. Tags <h1> through <h3> should all contain the primary keyword spaced throughout the page with the <h1> and <h2> tags being above the Website fold.

Internal Link – Internal links are links from your page's content to another page or section on the same domain. Internal links are important when it comes to On-Site SEO as discussed in Chapter 4.

Keyword – A keyword is a word or phrase that is used to optimize a Website or Webpage. Selecting keywords is one of the most important tasks in SEO work and selecting the right keywords in the outset can either make or break you. It's important to note that the keyword "Miami vacation" and "vacation Miami" will produce different search results, so the order and positioning of the words within the phrase is just as important.

Keyword Density – The keyword density is the number of times a keyword appears on a page in relation to the total number of words. Optimal keyword density ranges from 2% to 5% with anything considerably over 5% being construed as SPAM and anything considerably lower than

2% being construed as not keyword rich enough and thus less relevant. It's important when writing your content that your primary keyword is evenly distributed throughout the page, making sure that it appears in the first and last sentence of the content as well as evenly spaced throughout the balance of the words.

Keyword Stuffing – Keyword stuffing is the over usage of a keyword in content or meta keyword tags, something that used to be popular many years ago, but is now frowned upon as a Black-Hat SEO technique. Keyword stuffing is achieved in various different ways which include placing the phrase multiple times within the Meta tags while combined with other words in different combinations, applying the same color to the keywords as the background making them invisible, using the <noscript> tag, and using CSS z-positioning. All of these practices will get you demoted and sometimes de-indexed by search engines like Google.

Long Tail Keyword – A long tail keyword is a keyword that has a minimum of at least 3 words and any maximum number of words. Long tail keywords are used by marketers trying to target a specific niche, question or topic, which produce near similar results to a broader search term of lessor keywords but may have higher competition. Long tail keywords are a great way to rank at the top of search engine results for terms that may otherwise be more difficult to rank for.

Link Bait – Link Bait refers to content that is created in order to garner as many links to it as possible. Since backlinks are one of the primary drivers of SERP positioning, many SEO efforts include the creation of content with the primary goal to get as many links back to that content as possible.

Link Farm – A link farm is a group of sites that all hyperlink to one another, back and forth in an oscillating fashion. While link farms used to be advantageous, they don't have large relevancy today since the two-way links make it confusing for search engines to determine which site is the vendor and which is the promoting site.

Link Juice – This is the SEO linking power of a page and usually refers to the combined sum of the link power of all the pages linking into it. You'll hear the term link juice referenced when quantifying the power of a certain link or a page that those links lead to.

Link Pyramid – A Link Pyramid is a very powerful form of Off-Site SEO backlinking that involves the creation of a linking structure that is extremely powerful. Think of the strength in physical form that a real pyramid has and how the transference of force is physically supported by the structure itself and how that has stood the test of time. Link Pyramids generally have three tiers: a bottom tier with low level links, a middle with medium level links, and a top level with high level EDU, GOV or other authority links. The bottom links link to the middle, the middle links link to the top, and the top links link to your site.

Link Sculpting – When you implement attributes to links

to affect their behavior in how search engines interpret them, you're engaging in link sculpting. The most common form of link sculpting is using the Nofollow or Dofollow link sculpting forms. The Nofollow links tell a search engine not to follow a link, thus leaving the link juice on the page, while a Dofollow link tells a search engine to continue on to follow that link thus disseminating the link juice to the next page.

Link Wheel – A Link Wheel is a form of linking that links one site to another while also linking back to your site as well. The links flow in a sort of wheel format with the spokes being links back to your site in the center. When done correctly, a link wheel can be a powerful form of SEO boost for your Website and the most effective forms of link wheels are organically fashioned ones that utilize social media platforms as their linking mediums.

Meta Keywords – Meta keywords are part of a set of Meta Tags that appear in the header of Websites. Meta keywords used to be prominently used in search engine rankings but have no interpreted value of importance today. Instead of using meta keywords, search algorithms now use other tags such as heading tags, site content, keyword density and backlinking keywords to determine search engine rankings.

Meta Description – The meta description tag is one of the meta tags that are still used by search engines to display search results. This along with the title tag is used to display the name and description of the link on SERPs to the user searching for information.

Nofollow Links – Search engines spider the Web looking for information and in turn ranking the relevance of sites in its indexes. Nofollow links are an HTML attribute associated with hyper links that tell a search engine to not follow the link, stopping the search engine's traffic at that page, almost like a dead end. Nofollow links are optimal when it comes to making sure that your own page is optimized to the highest level possible by not allowing the link juice to pass through it.

Off-Site SEO – Off-Site SEO are the methods and practices of performing SEO work that happen away from the site itself. Off-Site SEO mainly involves the use of heavy backlinking, social media shares, authority site content creation (i.e. squidoo.com, youtube.com, etc.), article spinning, and so on. Off-Site SEO is a very labor-intensive part of the SEO trade and I've dedicated an entire chapter to it to help you efficiently tackle it without wasting your efforts and making mistakes.

On-site SEO – Any work that is done on the Website to increase the effectiveness of its SEO is considered On-Site SEO. This includes any HTML work, content creation, internal linking, setup, keyword distribution, and other related efforts.

Page Title – The HTML page title is the descriptive site title detail that resides within the page's <title> tags. This information is displayed by the search engines and is used in ranking the site on the SERPs. A good page title tag should be descriptive but not superfluous and should accomplish its goal in around 70 characters (the cut off point for most SERPs) with the use of the primary keyword.

Pinging – Pinging is a technique that notifies the search engines to go out and seek data from a URL. This is required because a lot of the link building that is done happens on low, or no page rank sites that do not get visited often or at all by the search engines. When a search engine is pinged to go out and index a URL you can be certain that the hyperlink to your site or to another link in a link pyramid that's pointing to your site, will be found and indexed.

Panda – The Google Panda is a change in the algorithm for Google's search results that was released in February of 2011. The effects of Panda were to demote low quality sites and promote sites with high quality well researched information. The effects of this release were widespread, making huge shifts in positioning on SERPs forcing some businesses to lose large volumes of search traffic while others were able to gain it.

Page Rank – One of the most important descriptors of a Web page, the page rank is a Web page's rank in relevancy on the Internet, ranging from 0 to 10. Sites like Facebook, Twitter, and Google's home page achieve Page ranks of 9 and 10, while lower trafficked sites have lesser page ranks.

Penguin – The Google Penguin was one of the latest major updates released to Google's algorithm on April

24th, 2012, that began to demote visibility of listings on SERPs that violated Google's Webmaster guidelines and employed Black-Hat SEO tactics such as cloaking, keyword stuffing, and the creation of duplicate content.

PPC - Pay-per-click advertising, or PPC, is a form of paid search engine advertising that marketers use to get their message out to the masses on a large scale very quickly. PPC ads show up on the right side of SERPs and are now also being implemented on Facebook, YouTube videos, and more recently on sites like Twitter.

PPV – Pay per view ads, or PPV, is a type of advertising that is utilized by marketers to distribute ads to a user base that has expressly agreed to receive those ads. An example of this is free software downloads or online services such as Pandora that use PPV ads to display advertisements on a periodic basis while providing a free service.

Referrer String – Referrer strings are used in affiliate and Web marketing to pinpoint campaigns and where a lead or referral came from. This is important to some marketers running paid advertisements to be able to gauge the successes of their various efforts throughout the Web. Web programming dictates that after the Web page name, a question mark can indicate the start of any variables that may be appended to a URL, thus resulting in a Referrer String.

Robots.txt – This is a file that resides in the root directory of your Website, that provides instructions to search engines on any folders, or files that it shouldn't index. Most people don't want search engines seeing all files on their sites such as administration files, or other files that contain sensitive information.

RSS Feed – A Rich Site Summary (RSS) feed is a standardized format that allows for the automatic update and syndication of content on sites that have frequent changes and entries such as blogs and other news sites. The RSS feed format provides a standard in formatting that allows ease of redistribution of either full or summarized data, metadata and publishing information.

Sandbox – Google Sandbox Effect is an effect that happens when a newly formed domain name's link juice is not fully weighted due to filtering from Google in order to prevent SPAMMERS from reaching the first page in SERPs by registering multiple domain names quickly and actively promoting them.

Search Algorithm – A formula devised by brilliant minds that weighs and takes multiple factors into account when reaching a determination for search result page ranking. The Google search algorithm combines many factors including the aged domain factor, Website link popularity, On-Site SEO elements, and Off-Site SEO elements. No one outside of Google knows the exact current algorithm and the total weight of each of the factors that are taken into account or precisely how they impact search results but there are very good guidelines available.

SEM – SEM is the business of search engine marketing, the industry that search engine optimization specialists fall under. SEM is used to refer to not only SEO efforts but also paid search engine marketing efforts as well.

SERP – Search Engine Ranking Pages, also known as SERPs, are the end listing results pages of queries to search engines. SERPs will generally include a title and brief description of each listing related to the keywords searched along with a link to that content. In SEO the goal is to dominate the first page of SERPs.

Sitemap – A sitemap is a page that's created to aid browsers in crawling a site. A sitemap provides a hierarchical link structure of pages on a Website that are accessible and permissible to be crawled.

Social Media – Social media is a term that refers to the types of sites that have increased in popularity in the past several years that base themselves on end user interactions in a social and collaborative format. Examples of such popular sites are Facebook, Google Plus, and Twitter.

Spider – A Spider is a Web-robot that's instructed to go out and crawl the Internet for data used for the purposes of Website indexing and rankings. Google has multiple spiders that it sends out, some that are dedicated to deep-indexing the Web, others for more periodic updates to Web content, and even others for algorithm adjustments such as the Google Panda and Google Penguin.

Website Fold – The Website fold is the section of the Website that is viewable to the natural eye prior to getting cut off by the browser and forcing a user to scroll. The Website fold will vary from screen resolution to screen resolution, however it's typically 600 to 850 pixels down from the top of the browser.

White-Hat SEO – White-Hat SEO techniques are those that follow the rules and standards of the SEO world and also adhere to Google's Webmaster Guidelines. White-Hat SEO techniques, while more time intensive, offer the largest long-term gains for your Website's ranking on SERPs. These techniques include quality content creation, proper On-Site SEO configuration, and organically looking Off-Site SEO linking.

26494282R00096

Made in the USA
Lexington, KY
03 October 2013